Kolyma

The Frozen Hell of Stalin's Siberian Gulags

Hourglass History

Table of Contents

CHAPTER 1

The Enigma of Kolyma

The vast stretches of the Siberian tundra have always seemed infinite, its cold plains spreading out beneath a churning sky, interminable and forbidding. Into this isolated realm, many great empires and adventurous souls have ventured, seeking either dominion or escape, often encountering a ruthless adversary far stronger than any human enemy: nature itself. Yet, few regions of Siberia carry the burden of history as heavily as Kolyma. A name that, in certain circles, reverberates with a bone-chilling echo, evoking memories of a past that still casts its shadow over the present.

History is often most profoundly felt in places where silence prevails. Silence, that envelops the land like a shroud. This is true for Kolyma, where the stillness is punctuated only by the whisper of wind through the trees and the haunting calls of distant wildlife. But the land, seemingly untouched and pristine, carries a weight. Its soil, frozen for most of the year, conceals the narratives of countless souls, many of whom came here involuntarily, ensnared in a web of political intrigue, suspicion, and, at times, sheer caprice.

To comprehend Kolyma is not merely to recount dates and figures or to trace the routes of prisoner transports on a map. It is to delve deep into the psyche of an era, to attempt to understand how a society, fresh with revolutionary fervor, intent on building a new world, could create its own heart of darkness in such a remote corner of the earth.

For much of its existence, Kolyma remained terra incognita to the Russian imagination. Lying in the northeastern extremities of Siberia, it was, for all intents and purposes, off the map. It was only during the 20th century, with the rise of the Soviet Union and its insatiable thirst for resources and control, that Kolyma was thrust into prominence. In the broader annals of Russian history, it might be seen as a blink. But what a profound and tumultuous blink it was.

Under the vast Siberian sky, where the boundaries between day and night blur during summers and winters, Kolyma was both a dream and a nightmare. For the state, it was a dream of wealth and potential, with its untapped deposits of gold and other valuable minerals. It was an opportunity for the young Soviet Union to demonstrate its dominion over nature, to show that it could harness even the most hostile environments to further its revolutionary cause. But for the tens of thousands who would be exiled here, it was a nightmare. The unrelenting cold, the grueling labor, and the omnipresent specter of death turned the dream of a socialist utopia into an icy hell.

It's tempting to view Kolyma merely as a place, a geographic entity characterized by its longitudes, latitudes, and mineral deposits. But to do so would be to rob it of its depth. For Kolyma is not just a place, it's a chapter in the human saga, one that speaks to the complexities and paradoxes of the 20th century. A time when humanity reached new pinnacles of achievement, but also plumbed new depths of cruelty.

The gravity of Kolyma's past is evident in the silence that surrounded it for decades. The Soviet state, always keen to control its own narrative, was equally adept at erasing the stories it found inconvenient. In the vast expanse of the USSR's history books, Kolyma was often reduced to a footnote, its true significance obscured beneath layers of official jargon and omissions.

Yet, history, much like the resilient larch trees that dot the Siberian landscape, has a way of enduring. The stories of Kolyma, though suppressed, never truly disappeared. They lingered, whispered from generation to generation, preserved in letters, diaries, and the memories of those who survived. And now, as we embark on this journey into the heart of Siberia, we must approach it with the respect and gravity it deserves.

For Kolyma is not just a testament to the human capacity for cruelty, but also to the indomitable spirit of those who endured, resisted, and remembered. It serves as a reminder that history is not just about the movements of armies or the decrees of leaders. It's about the lived experiences of individuals, the choices they make, and the legacies they leave behind. In the silent vastness of Kolyma, we find a microcosm of the human experience, in all its complexities, tragedies, and triumphs.

CHAPTER 2

Siberia's Dreaded Landscape

The vastness of Siberia is almost incomprehensible to the human mind. Stretching over seven million square miles, it sprawls across one-eighth of the world's landmass, dwarfing entire nations with its size. And yet, its population has always remained scant, inhibited by a landscape that, in its sheer indifference, veers on hostility.

To truly appreciate the forbidding nature of Siberia, one must first disabuse oneself of any romantic notions that might have been conceived by reading the adventure tales of old. The realities faced by explorers, convicts, and latterly, the victims of political purges, were far from the fantastical journeys depicted in books. This is a land where nature, raw and untamed, is in eternal command.

The Siberian climate is often the first adversary any traveler or resident encounters. Its winters are the stuff of legend – long, mercilessly cold, with temperatures often plummeting to minus fifty degrees Celsius or even lower. The air turns so brittle that it feels like it might shatter. Exhale, and one's breath becomes a visible mist, crystallizing instantly. Unprotected skin can freeze within minutes, leading to the dreaded frostbite that has claimed many a limb.

But to fixate only on the cold would be to overlook Siberia's paradoxical nature. For it isn't a perennial wasteland of snow. Its summers, though brief, can be surprisingly warm, with temperatures occasionally soaring to thirty degrees Celsius. This dramatic fluctuation, however, brings its own set of challenges. The frozen ground, or permafrost, begins to thaw, turning vast tracts of land into muddy, impassable swamps. The thick, impenetrable forests, or taigas, become infested with mosquitoes and other insects, turning every venture into a torment.

Beyond the taigas lie the tundras, vast plains where the ground remains permanently frozen. Trees become sparse, replaced by hardy shrubs and mosses that eke out an existence in this desolate expanse. The winds here carry no obstruction, sweeping the plains with an unyielding force that chills to the bone.

Navigating this terrain has always been challenging. Before the advent of modern transportation, journeys were undertaken by foot or on horseback during the brief summer months. During winter, sleds drawn by dogs or reindeer would traverse the frozen rivers, which provided the smoothest routes through the rugged landscape. However, such journeys were not without peril. The ice could crack without warning, swallowing up entire sled teams. Blizzards could rise suddenly, disorienting travelers and burying them beneath snowdrifts.

The indigenous peoples of Siberia, such as the Evenks, Nenets, and Yakuts, had, over millennia, adapted to these harsh conditions. Their nomadic lifestyles, centered around reindeer herding or hunting, were in harmony with the seasonal rhythms of the land. They had mastered the art of survival in an environment that offered little room for error. Every aspect of their lives, from their clothing made of reindeer fur to their portable tents, or yurts, was optimized for survival.

However, for outsiders, Siberia was, and to some extent still is, a realm of dread. The very name became synonymous with exile and suffering. For the tsarist regime and later the Soviet Union, its remoteness and harshness made it an ideal location for penal colonies. The environment itself was a prison, with the vast distances and inhospitable terrain acting as formidable barriers to escape.

The sheer scale of Siberia also made it a place of mystery. Many areas remained uncharted until the late 19th and early 20th centuries. Local legends spoke of strange creatures that roamed the forests and mystical spirits that guarded sacred sites. Even today, Siberia retains an aura of the unknown, with many areas still largely uninhabited and untouched by modern civilization.

Yet, despite its challenges, Siberia is not without its beauty. The Northern Lights, or Aurora Borealis, turn the night sky into a mesmerizing dance of colors. The vast, pristine landscapes, whether the dense taigas or the open tundras, have a stark beauty that can be profoundly moving. Lakes like Baikal, the deepest in the world, hold mysteries and stories of their own.

Moreover, Siberia is not a static entity. Over the millennia, its landscapes have evolved, shaped by the forces of nature. Glaciers advanced and retreated, carving out valleys and shaping mountains. Rivers changed their courses, creating new pathways through the wilderness. And the flora and fauna, from the mighty Siberian tiger to the delicate edelweiss flower, found ways to thrive against the odds.

The land also bears the scars of human activity. Over the centuries, fires, both natural and man-made, have ravaged its forests. Mining activities, especially during the Soviet era, left indelible marks on the landscape. And the infrastructure of the Gulag system, of which Kolyma was a significant part, introduced new settlements, roads, and industries to the hinterland.

To understand Kolyma, it's essential to grasp Siberia's character, for the two are intrinsically linked. Kolyma was not an anomaly but a product of its environment, shaped by the very land upon which it was built. It stood as a testament to humanity's relentless quest for dominion, even in the face of nature's might.

But as history would show, Siberia, with all its vastness and ferocity, was not just a passive backdrop. It played an active role in the stories of those who ventured into its depths, whether willingly or by force. It was both a witness and a participant, its character woven indelibly into the tapestry of their lives. And as the narrative of Kolyma unfolds, Siberia's shadow, both majestic and menacing, looms large over every page.

CHAPTER 3

The Origins of the Gulag System

In the cataclysmic aftermath of the 1917 Revolution, Russia's map was reconfigured not merely in political borders but in a more insidious way: the contours of control. Even as the country lay battered by civil war, famine, and the turbulence of creating a new political order, its leaders were already envisaging a system to consolidate power. That system would eventually evolve into the notorious Gulag.

The term "Gulag" is an acronym for Glavnoe Upravlenie Lagerei, or the Main Administration of Camps. But this bureaucratic denomination belies the chilling reality it would soon embody. Long before Kolyma became a byword for suffering, the foundations of the Soviet Union's prison camp system were being laid.

Lenin, the vanguard of the Bolshevik Revolution, believed in the importance of isolating "counter-revolutionaries" and "enemies of the people" for both punitive and re-educational purposes. The newly established All-Russian Extraordinary Commission for Combating Counter-Revolution and Sabotage, or Cheka, took this directive with alarming zeal. By 1919, concentration camps, a phenomenon Europe had already seen during World War I, began to appear across Soviet territory. These initial camps, however, were ad hoc, decentralized, and often temporary.

What prompted the shift from these rudimentary camps to a vast, systematic network? The answer lies in the complex interplay of politics, ideology, and economy. Lenin, despite his revolutionary fervor, was not blind to the dire straits of the Soviet economy. Russia, once a major world producer of commodities like timber and gold, had seen a catastrophic decline in its output. The Civil War had devastated infrastructure, displaced millions, and ground industries to a halt.

For Lenin, the camps were a potential solution to both the political threat of dissent and the economic imperative of reconstruction. In 1921, he issued a directive emphasizing the economic utility of the prisoner workforce. The very next year, the Soviet government approved the establishment of the All-Russian Camp Administration, which, while still modest in scope, signaled a conceptual shift from merely punitive camps to ones that would combine punishment with economic productivity.

But the camps' transformation into an economic juggernaut would be fully realized under Joseph Stalin. As Lenin's health declined and his involvement in the daily affairs of the state diminished, Stalin began to consolidate power. By the late 1920s, his position was unassailable. With it came a vision for Russia, one marked by rapid industrialization and the collectivization of agriculture, encapsulated in the Five-Year Plans. This vision, however, required resources – both material and human.

The first major expansion of the camp system under Stalin came in the late 1920s with the Shakhty trial. Accused of conspiring with foreign powers to sabotage the Soviet coal industry, several engineers were sentenced to death, while many others faced long prison sentences. The event was less about the purported sabotage and more a demonstration of Stalin's intentions: no one, irrespective of their stature, was beyond the state's reach. And the result? The emergence of labor camps specifically designed to harness the expertise of the convicted specialists.

The 1930s would see the system expand exponentially. The dual drive of industrialization and the battle against perceived "enemies" saw camps sprouting across the vast expanses of the Soviet Union, from the icy tundras of the Arctic to the dense forests of Siberia. But these weren't mere prisons; they were vast economic enterprises. Forests were felled for timber, mines were dug for precious metals, and canals were constructed to alter the flow of rivers. The workforce behind these monumental tasks? Millions of incarcerated souls.

However, it wasn't just economic imperatives that fueled the growth of the Gulags. The ideological construct of the Soviet state placed a significant emphasis on the re-education of its prisoners. These were not just camps; they were, in theory, 'corrective labor colonies'. The idea was that through hard labor, the "corrupt" elements of the society – be it the bourgeoisie, religious leaders, nationalists, or later, even perceived political dissenters – would be transformed into productive, obedient Soviet citizens.

This ideological underpinning is essential to understanding the Gulag's nature. It wasn't just a place of punishment; it was a crucible in which a new Soviet identity was to be forged. Of course, the reality was often far removed from this ideal. The conditions in many of the camps were brutal, with prisoners often subjected to grueling labor, inadequate food, and extreme weather conditions.

Yet, even in these early years, the Gulag system was not monolithic. Camps varied in their size, purpose, and conditions. Some, particularly those housing political prisoners or intellectuals, had better facilities, while others, meant for criminals or perceived 'lower elements', were notoriously harsh.

The rise of the Gulag system is a testament to the entwining of political ambition, economic exigency, and ideological fervor. The camps became a symbol of the state's power, its ability to mobilize resources, human or otherwise, for its grand vision. But they were also a chilling reminder of the cost of dissent in Stalin's Russia. As the Gulag's grip tightened, and its tentacles spread further, it set the stage for one of the darkest chapters in human history, a chapter in which Kolyma would become a stark emblem of both human endurance and cruelty.

CHAPTER 4

Stalin's Iron Grip and the Purges

In a world reconfigured by the promise of a new socialist order, Joseph Stalin emerged not as a guardian of the collective dream but rather its tyrant. With his regime, Russia underwent a phase where the state's machinery was unforgiving, where dissent was synonymous with disappearance, and where paranoia manifested in wide-scale purges that consumed the very people it promised to champion.

Emerging from the shadows of Lenin's leadership, Stalin did not merely inherit the Soviet system; he remolded it with a determination that was both steely and macabre. There were, of course, critical decisions made under Lenin's aegis which laid the foundational bricks for the expansive Gulag system, including the inception of concentration camps for counter-revolutionaries. But it was under Stalin that these mechanisms burgeoned and became the very scaffolding of Soviet governance.

Stalin's Soviet Union bore the emblems of modernity: industrialization at a pace that left the Western world both astonished and anxious, with glittering cities sprouting like mirages in the vastness of Russia's hinterland. The First Five-Year Plan, initiated in 1928, was a testament to this rapid industrial metamorphosis, setting aggressive targets for the sectors of coal, iron, and electricity. With all eyes on the future, few dared to voice a pivotal concern: at what cost does progress come?

The answer lay, starkly, in the lives and liberties of the Soviet people. Those who were branded as enemies of the state, a perilous label with ever-shifting definitions, found themselves ensnared in a web of intrigue, surveillance, and betrayal. The purges of the 1930s, often referred to as the "Great Terror," were not simply random manifestations of Stalin's paranoia but were deeply rooted in a strategy designed to consolidate power.

Two pivotal elements defined Stalin's reign of terror: the purges and the show trials. Both were tools of propaganda, a means to reaffirm state authority and, paradoxically, to sow seeds of uncertainty amongst the masses.

By 1934, the assassination of Sergei Kirov, a prominent Bolshevik leader, became the lightning rod that intensified Stalin's campaign against perceived counter-revolutionaries. Even though the actual circumstances surrounding Kirov's death remain enigmatic, it was presented as a conspiracy, thereby justifying widespread arrests. What followed was an avalanche of purges that engulfed party members, military officers, intelligentsia, and ordinary citizens. As historian Robert Conquest noted, no one was safe from the scythe of suspicion.

Yet, the purges weren't merely about removing potential threats. They also played an economic role. The surge of arrests meant an influx of forced labor, a convenient reservoir of manpower for the state's ambitious infrastructural projects, including the construction of the White Sea-Baltic Canal.

Stalin's purges, however, were not limited to the anonymous masses. They extended their chilling fingers into the very heart of the Bolshevik elite. The Party Congresses, once a platform for intellectual debate, had, by the mid-1930s, morphed into orchestrated events. The 1934 Congress, known as the Congress of Victors, is particularly illustrative. Out of its 1,966 delegates, 1,108 would later be arrested, their contributions erased, their existences rendered void.

But arrests were just the first step in a meticulously choreographed dance of oppression. The show trials that began in 1936 were public spectacles, theatre where the conclusions were preordained. Old Bolshevik stalwarts like Grigory Zinoviev and Lev Kamenev were paraded, their confessions – often extracted under extreme duress or the promise of leniency – broadcasted as evidence of vast counter-revolutionary conspiracies.

While these trials were ostensibly aimed at rooting out Trotskyists and other "enemies" within the party, their real purpose was twofold. Firstly, they were a cautionary tale, an assertion of the inescapability of the state's gaze. Secondly, they were a means to rewrite history, to sculpt a narrative that placed Stalin at the heart of the revolution, sidelining figures like Trotsky, who was airbrushed from photographs, banished from Soviet historiography.

The state machinery was bolstered by the NKVD (People's Commissariat for Internal Affairs), under the leadership of the infamous Nikolai Yezhov. This period, often called the Yezhovshchina, saw the NKVD not merely as an instrument of the state but almost as a parallel entity, its power so pervasive that it consumed even its own. By 1938, Yezhov himself fell from grace, replaced by Lavrentiy Beria, but the machinery of repression he'd overseen continued its relentless grind.

Yet, the scale of the purges, the sheer numbers arrested, tried, or executed, does not solely define their horror. It's the everydayness of betrayal they engendered. Neighbors informed on neighbors, colleagues on colleagues, sometimes family on family. This climate of mutual distrust was perhaps the most insidious legacy of Stalin's purges. As writer Alexander Solzhenitsyn would later pen in 'The Gulag Archipelago', the line dividing good and evil cuts through every human heart, and Stalin's reign rendered that line perilously thin.

By the late 1930s, the purges began to wane, not out of benevolence, but out of necessity. The looming threat of Nazi Germany meant that Stalin needed a cohesive state, a united front. The Molotov-Ribbentrop Pact of 1939, a non-aggression treaty with Nazi Germany, bought the Soviet Union time, but it was a lull before the storm.

In retrospect, Stalin's purges appear as a paradox: an attempt to solidify the state by tearing apart its very fabric. The legacy of the purges, though, is not simply in the numbers they consumed or the terror they sowed, but in the narrative they constructed. A narrative where the state was both protector and predator, where history was malleable, and where the cost of silence, of complicity, was etched into the frozen landscapes of places like Kolyma, a testament to the fragility and resilience of the human spirit.

CHAPTER 5:

Construction of a Frozen Hell

As we journey back in time, within the biting landscape of Siberia, the birth of a man-made nightmare was unfurling. The very terrain seemed to challenge human endeavors, but for Joseph Stalin and his regime, this land, as bleak and unyielding as it was, held the perfect isolation for the Kolyma labor camps. It was in this vast, desolate landscape that the Soviet Union began the formidable construction of what would become one of the most infamous penal colonies in history.

The Kolyma River, coursing through Northeastern Siberia, bestowed its name upon this chain of camps. The river, like an undeterred force of nature, traversed an area nearly seven times the size of France, coursing through regions untouched by civilization, hostile even to native fauna. Yet, the very hostility of this place rendered it ideal for its proposed purpose.

The nature of these camps was dual: they were both prison and gold mine. The Soviet State had always been cognizant of Siberia's rich, natural resources, but harnessing these in the wilderness required a mammoth workforce. Who better to exploit than enemies of the state, real or imagined? It was a pernicious equation: political containment meets economic ambition.

The first shovels that broke the frozen ground were not held by machinery or free workers but by emaciated hands. These early prisoners, perhaps artists or thinkers in a life not long past, were reduced to mere physical tools. But these weren't mere foundations for buildings; they were laying down the substructure of a system that would consume countless lives.

Engineering such a place in Siberia's remoteness was no small feat. The earth was like iron, frozen deep, requiring constant labor to pierce. Yet, the initial establishments were rudimentary, transient almost. Tent cities arose, mere canvases flapping against the icy wind. Yet, these canvases, bleak as they were, would be homes for many. Only gradually, with the influx of more prisoners, were permanent wooden barracks constructed.

Fuel and resources were scarce. Trees, sparse and stunted from the unforgiving cold, were felled by malnourished prisoners. Transported logs became the skeletal frames for the camps. It's uncanny, isn't it? How an environment so devoid of life became the very bedrock of an institution built on suffering?

As more camps were built, a macabre routine emerged. Those in earlier camps, despite their weakened states, were forced to construct railways to connect the new ones. This ever-expanding web of tracks facilitated the movement of guards, prisoners, and most crucially, the mined gold.

Kolyma wasn't just about isolation; it was strategic, too. The region was rich in not only gold but also coal, tin, and other minerals. The establishment of the town of Magadan in 1930 by the Dalstroy, a state-owned construction trust, marked the formal initiation of the region's exploitation. Entrusted to harness Kolyma's treasures, Dalstroy, under Eduard Berzin's leadership, oversaw the establishment of roads, ports, and mines, transforming the inhospitable land into an industrial hub.

Magadan, the gateway to Kolyma, bore witness to Dalstroy's prowess. Buildings, not merely functional but also representing a certain grandeur, rose, echoing Moscow's architectural aesthetics. Yet, the town's urban veneer thinly veiled the torment beneath. It was here that the prisoners were processed, cataloged like objects, stripped of their humanity before being dispatched deeper into the abyss.

Remarkably, though many parts of Kolyma were essentially unreachable for parts of the year due to the intense cold and the absence of roads, the Soviets pressed on. Laborers, under constant surveillance, toiled day and night, dynamiting the permafrost to forge paths. The so-called 'Road of Bones,' built by the prisoners, is a grim testament to this period, said to contain the remains of those who perished during its construction.

The infrastructure was not just about exploitation but also containment. Guard towers, intimidating and ever-watchful, rose high. Double-perimeter fences, entwined with barbed wire, ensured that the vast wilderness outside was not a means of escape but an additional barrier. Dogs, as famished as the prisoners, were trained to be ruthless, ready to hunt down any potential escapee.

Every detail in the construction echoed a chilling efficiency. Even the camp's internal roads were designed to minimize the chance of revolts. They were narrow, ensuring prisoners marched in single file, watched from all angles by armed guards.

But it wasn't just about physical barriers. Psychological warfare was crucial in the architectural design. The camps' very layout, with commandant offices overlooking the barracks, fostered a sense of omnipresence. You were always watched, always under the state's shadow.

These architectural choices, dictated from desks in Moscow, bore testimony to a deeply ingrained ethos of the Stalinist regime: control was paramount. Whether through isolation, labor, or fear, the Soviet machinery was designed for unwavering dominance. The construction of Kolyma wasn't just about building camps; it was about forging chains that not even the vast expanse of Siberia could break.

The air in Kolyma was dense with more than just the cold. It was laden with despair, with the knowledge that this remote land, once indifferent to human existence, had been violently transformed. The barracks, roads, and mines stood not just as symbols of Soviet ambition but as monuments to human suffering, as gravestones for countless souls.

In the end, the construction of Kolyma was not just an architectural endeavor; it was a chilling testament to the lengths to which a regime could go to maintain control and drive progress. The dual purpose of these camps, both as prisons and as centers of economic extraction, showcased the dark efficiency of the Soviet system, where human lives were mere cogs in a larger, merciless machine.

CHAPTER 6:

The Quest for Gold and Resources

The frozen landscapes of Kolyma held secrets that went far beyond its chilling exterior. Beneath its desolate surface lay veins of gold, pockets of platinum, and other valuable resources. Kolyma, despite its hellish conditions for prisoners, glittered in the eyes of Stalin's regime, promising wealth that could finance the ambitions of a vast empire.

The Soviet Union's early years were fraught with challenges: Civil War, foreign intervention, and an economy on the brink of collapse. In the depths of such despair, gold became an emblem of hope, a tangible asset that could propel the USSR to world prominence. And where better to find it than in the untapped vastness of the Russian Far East? Kolyma became the theater of a dual narrative - one of forced labor and inhumane treatment and the other of the country's quest for gold and economic dominance.

Geologists had long suspected that this northeastern region held immense mineral wealth, though its inaccessibility and the challenges posed by its harsh climate had discouraged exploration. But the Soviet leadership, desperate to harness every resource to establish their nation as a global powerhouse, was undeterred by such obstacles. This was a regime that dreamt big, with grand designs of colossal dams, vast industrial complexes, and endless railways. To realize these dreams, money was needed, and that meant gold.

In the 1930s, the first expeditions to Kolyma reported findings that exceeded expectations. The deposits of gold were vast, possibly among the largest globally. But as news of the discovery spread, so too did an awareness of the challenges of extracting it. The ground was permanently frozen, tools were rudimentary, and the weather could make any form of work near impossible. Yet these very challenges made Kolyma the ideal site for the Gulag system. It was a place where a seemingly endless supply of forced labor could be deployed to extract gold at any cost.

Severely ill-equipped for such a massive undertaking, laborers – political prisoners, intellectuals, and common criminals alike – were given the barest of tools: pans, shovels, and often just their bare hands, to dig into the permafrost. The conditions were backbreaking. In the winter, the ground turned to iron, resisting every blow. In the summer, the brief thaw turned everything to mud, creating treacherous pits that could swallow a man whole.

But the economics of it were brutally simple. The human cost was disregarded entirely. Prisoners were expendable, and there was always a fresh supply of labor. In this relentless pursuit of gold, the average life expectancy of a Kolyma miner was a mere few months.

Yet, as the years progressed, the amount of gold extracted from Kolyma began to reach staggering proportions. By some estimates, during the peak years, the region was responsible for up to a fifth of the world's total gold production. This gold filled the Soviet coffers, funded industrial projects, and ensured the USSR's solvency in international markets.

But gold was not the only prize. Kolyma had other treasures too: tin, silver, and platinum, and even coal reserves. These materials became essential components of Stalin's ambitions, feeding the Soviet industrial machine.

The focus on gold extraction also brought about a hierarchy within the camp system. Those who were assigned to the gold mines were at once the most unfortunate and the most critical in the eyes of the Soviet authorities. They worked under the harshest conditions but were also subject to the strictest production quotas. Failure to meet these quotas often meant reduced rations or even execution, making every day a desperate race against time and exhaustion.

Yet, the sheer scale of the operation and its importance to the Soviet state meant that it was also a place of innovation, albeit driven by necessity rather than humanistic considerations. The permafrost that made mining so challenging was also employed as an asset. Since it was impossible to dig traditional mineshafts, the miners would extract the gold from the surface, creating vast, open-pit mines. These became scars on the landscape, a testament to the scale of the operation.

As the gold flowed from Kolyma to Moscow, there was little regard for the hands that had extracted it. The state propaganda hailed the monumental achievements of Soviet industry and the indomitable spirit of its workers. There was no mention of the thousands who had died in the process or the forced labor that underpinned the entire operation.

In the grand narrative of Soviet progress, Kolyma's gold was a symbol of the nation's triumph over adversity. But for those who toiled in its mines, it was a grim reminder of the human cost of such ambitions. The glint of gold, so promising on the surface, masked a dark underbelly of exploitation and suffering.

And so, as the world marveled at the Soviet Union's rapid industrialization and the strength of its economy, few realized that the gleam of its wealth had its origins in the frozen wastelands of Kolyma. Here, in the most inhospitable of environments, the USSR had found its El Dorado. But this city of gold had been built not on the dreams of adventurers but on the broken backs of its prisoners.

Kolyma's gold, extracted at such a high human cost, would forever remain a testament to the dualities of the Soviet project: extraordinary achievements and unimaginable suffering, side by side. It was a story of riches and ruin, of a nation's golden dreams and the dark realities that underpinned them.

CHAPTER 7

The Journey: Transporting Prisoners to the Edge

In Stalin's regime, Siberia, and more pointedly Kolyma, became a vast, frigid and unyielding home for the many deemed unworthy or dangerous to the Soviet system. But before they would confront the biting cold, the unending labor, and the despair of Kolyma's camps, they had to get there.

The transportation of prisoners to Kolyma is not a journey that history ought to recall with nonchalance. It was not merely a process of movement but an agonizing prologue to the horrors that lay ahead. The journey symbolized the slow stripping away of identity, of humanity, until what remained was an empty vessel of hopelessness, anticipating Kolyma's unforgiving embrace.

For many, the journey began with an arrest, often abrupt and without clear cause. Secret police would knock on doors in the depth of night, spiriting away the accused, leaving behind only anguish and unanswered questions. The reasons varied: political dissent, religious beliefs, or sometimes the mere whisper of dissent, magnified in the ears of Stalin's ever-watchful informers.

Train stations, often bustling centers of life and commerce, became grim waypoints on the road to oblivion.

Cattle cars, not designed for human transportation but rather for livestock, became mobile prisons. Devoid of comfort or even basic amenities, these vehicles of despair bore their human cargo across the vast Russian landscape.

Inside, the prisoners found themselves in a world shorn of light and air. Bodies pressed against bodies in suffocating intimacy. A bucket in the corner, meant for waste, was a cruel testament to the complete degradation of dignity. The fetid smell, the anguished cries, the rustling of chains – these became the immediate sensory world of the prisoners.

And yet, within this infernal environment, glimmers of humanity still persisted. A mother might cradle her child, trying to shield the young one from the sight of a fellow prisoner, driven mad by thirst, licking the walls of the car for moisture. Some, armed only with stolen moments, scribbled words of resistance or simply chronicled the journey's agonies on scraps of paper, the walls of the car, or even on the soles of their shoes. In the midst of bleakness, they sought to document, to testify, to resist being forgotten.

The duration of the journey was torturous. Weeks transformed into months. As the train snaked its way through the Urals and into the vast expanse of Siberia, the outside world became a fleeting concept. Inside the cars, time lost its meaning. Days melded into nights, and despair into numbness.

Stops were infrequent, and when they did come, they offered no respite. Prisoners were often forced out into the snow for 'exercise', a cruel euphemism for moments of deeper degradation. These were opportunities for guards to exert their dominance, meting out punishment for perceived infractions or simply to alleviate their own boredom.

Food and water were scarce. The meager provisions that were distributed had to be fought over, reducing many to base instincts. Hunger gnawed at bellies and minds alike, fostering an environment where trust was luxury few could afford.

Despite the close quarters, isolation was a prisoner's constant companion. Rumors swirled about the ultimate destination. Some whispered of execution, while others clung to the hope of mere imprisonment. Most, however, had heard of Kolyma, its very name becoming synonymous with a frozen hell.

As the train rumbled forward, the landscape outside evolved. The greenery of European Russia gave way to the barren landscapes of Siberia, an ever-present reminder of the remoteness of their destination. Mountains loomed, rivers flowed, and forests sprawled – nature's vastness served as a stark contrast to the cramped confinement of the train cars.

But it wasn't just by train. Once the rail journey ended, often at Magadan or another port, many faced the additional ordeal of a sea voyage aboard ships, equally, if not more, harrowing. These vessels, ill-equipped for the transportation of humans, were battered by the stormy Sea of Okhotsk. Prisoners, already weakened from their rail ordeal, had to contend with seasickness, even more, cramped conditions, and the ever-present threat of being thrown overboard during storms.

Upon finally reaching their destination, the reality of their new existence began to dawn. For some, it was a sense of finality, a realization that this would be their last journey. For others, it was the beginning of a new nightmare, one that would test the very limits of their endurance.

The journey to Kolyma, harrowing in its cruelty, wasn't just a physical transition from one place to another. It was a transformation of the spirit. Stripped of identity, dignity, and hope, what arrived at Kolyma were not just prisoners, but shadows of their former selves, cast into the frozen depths of Stalin's most dreaded gulag.

And as history would note, this journey, in all its brutal simplicity, served as a chilling reminder of the lengths to which a regime could go to suppress, control, and dehumanize. The rickety trains, the frigid ships, the endless stretches of desolate landscape – they weren't just modes of transportation but instruments of terror, signaling to all the relentless might and cruelty of Stalin's Soviet Union.

CHAPTER 8

A Day in the Life: Kolyma's Brutal Routine

When one traverses the vast annals of history, the depths of human endurance are often delineated not in grand events, but in the mundane, the quotidian, and the painfully ordinary. It's in these routine moments that we glimpse the unvarnished spirit of a people and the true nature of their conditions. Kolyma, in the sweeping Soviet landscape, was more than a mere geographical entity; it was the embodiment of relentless suffering, marked most starkly in the day-to-day existence of its inmates.

A Kolyma morning was not greeted with the chirping of birds or a gentle rise of the sun. Instead, it was heralded by shrill whistles, the impatient clang of metal, and the cold dread that weighed down every heart. In the dim, pale light of the Siberian dawn, prisoners roused from their wooden bunks, the edges of which had often bitten into their skin as they slept. The air was pregnant with the acrid scent of human despair and sweat, mingling with the biting Siberian chill.

Breakfast, if one could call it that, was an exercise in humility. Each prisoner received a piece of hard, moldy bread, sometimes accompanied by a watery soup that held more promise in its steam than in its taste. For many, this would be the only meal before they embarked on hours of grueling labor. It was less a reprieve for hunger and more a ceremonial nod to the idea of sustenance. Conversations during this meager feast were terse, filled with an economy of words, each syllable carrying the weight of unspoken fears and subdued dreams.

Once the semblance of a meal was concluded, prisoners were hastily assembled into work brigades. The formation was a grim spectacle, a sea of gaunt faces and emaciated bodies, each bearing the mark of the indelible number that had replaced their identities. The guards, with a cold indifference that had become their hallmark, would count each inmate, ensuring none had escaped the drudgery of the day, or, more tragically, the confines of life itself.

The nature of the work varied, but the brutality was a constant. Gold mining, perhaps the most coveted of Kolyma's treasures, saw prisoners delving deep into the bowels of the earth, chipping away with rudimentary tools. The ground, stubbornly frozen, resisted their every effort. Each swing of the pickaxe, each shovelful of dirt, was a testament to man's unyielding spirit in the face of nature's cruelty. Others were set to tasks such as road construction, logging, or the construction of new camp facilities. Every endeavor seemed designed less for economic output and more for the grinding down of human souls.

Midday provided no respite. While the sun, a distant and indifferent observer, reached its zenith, the prisoners continued their labor. Lunch, when provided, was a repetition of breakfast, perhaps with the cruel addition of hope. Stories sometimes floated around – of a camp where the soup was thicker, or where an extra piece of bread was granted. But these tales were swallowed by the overwhelming reality that surrounded them.

As evening approached and shadows lengthened, the weary brigades would trudge back to the camps. Their bodies bore the marks of the day's toils – cuts, bruises, and sores. Yet, it was their eyes that told the true story. In them, one saw the reflections of crushed aspirations, memories of families left behind, and the haunting question of whether tomorrow would be a repetition of today or a release into the abyss of death.

Dinner was a mirror of previous meals, its monotony only broken occasionally by the allocation of a meager ration of horse meat or fish. Post the meal, the barracks became a theater of subdued activities. Some prisoners, still clinging to vestiges of their past lives, tried to read or write, their fingers trembling from cold and exhaustion. Others whispered stories or sang songs, their voices barely rising above the howling Siberian winds.

Nighttime was both a boon and a curse. While it provided a brief respite from labor, it also intensified the cold. Prisoners huddled together, seeking warmth in shared misery. Sleep, when it came, was fitful and fraught with nightmares, punctuated by the guards' sporadic inspections and the occasional cries of anguish from fellow inmates.

Such was a day in the life of a Kolyma inmate, a relentless cycle of labor, hunger, and cold. Yet, amidst this bleak routine, lay the indomitable human spirit – flickering, resilient, and waiting for dawn. For even in the darkest corners of history, hope has a way of piercing through, illuminating tales of endurance and courage that echo across time.

CHAPTER 9

Prisoner Hierarchies and Social Dynamics

In the heart of frozen Kolyma, a world removed from civilization, convicts didn't merely grapple with biting cold or the incessant labor that gnawed at their bones. They contended with a universe of social mores, distinctly fabricated by the walls of the camp and the people within. If Kolyma was a theater of tragedy, its prisoners were not merely its actors but also its unwitting playwrights, crafting a social script that would come to define existence in this Siberian outpost.

The tapestry of the Gulag's population was woven with strands of every color, texture, and pattern of Soviet society. Professors shared rations with pickpockets. Priests whispered prayers next to political dissidents. It would be easy, from a distance, to perceive these camps as levelers — places where the arbitrary distinctions of the 'free' world ceased to matter. But humans are a socially stratifying species, and the camps, even in their dehumanizing brutality, were no exception.

Within this confluence of disparate souls, a hierarchy emerged, not dissimilar to the hierarchies outside, but morphed and contorted by the peculiar pressures of camp life. The state had its official ranks, of course: camp administrators, guards, foremen. But amongst the prisoners, a more complex taxonomy developed, dictated as much by psychology as circumstance.

At the top were the blatnye, or criminal elite. The habitual offenders, they brought with them an understanding of prison dynamics from earlier stints in other detention facilities. These were the underworld bosses, the seasoned thieves, men and women who, paradoxically, seemed most at home in the incarcerating chill of Kolyma. They bore elaborate tattoos, each telling tales of criminal feats, allegiances, and time served. A lexicon of ink, these marks were a badge of pride, announcing their veteran status in this bleak world.

But it wasn't just tenure that placed the blatnye atop the prison food chain. It was an unwritten code: the ponyatiya, or thieves' law. This was a creed that scorned work and cooperation with authorities. For the blatnye, the true enemy wasn't necessarily the camp guard but the prisoner who sought compromise, who believed that hard work or obedience might earn him favor or an extra ration. To the blatnye, such behavior was treachery, a betrayal of the convict brotherhood.

Beneath the blatnye were the bytoviki, the common criminals. They lacked the status of the criminal elite, but they too adhered, at least nominally, to the ponyatiya. Theft, in this curious moral universe, was often lauded, a testament to one's cunning and resourcefulness. It was a perverse echo of the world outside, where cunning might win one a better job or a party promotion. Here, in the twisted mirror of Kolyma, it secured an extra piece of bread or a warmer pair of shoes.

The social landscape was further complicated by the politicheskiye, or political prisoners. These were the intellectuals, the dissidents, those who'd fallen foul of Stalin's ever-shifting ideological demands. Initially, they were treated with a modicum of respect, especially by the bytoviki. But as the 1930s wore on and the purges intensified, their numbers swelled, and with them, the contempt of the criminal class. The blatnye viewed them as soft, naive, lacking the streetwise savvy necessary for survival. The bytoviki, meanwhile, came to see them as competition, interlopers in an already crowded and hostile territory.

Yet, for all the friction, there was also solidarity. Common suffering birthed a shared humanity, a recognition that, whatever their past or station, they were all victims of the same merciless system. The politicheskiye, with their education and often noble ideals, set up makeshift classrooms, sharing their knowledge with those hungry for a glimpse of the world beyond the barbed wire.

Women, a minority in the camps, had their own hierarchical dynamics. While some achieved a kind of status through relationships with male criminals or guards, many more suffered doubly, victims not only of the Gulag's inherent cruelties but also of gendered violence. Still, they too found ways to forge bonds, to create pockets of mutual support in a universe that seemed to conspire against any semblance of hope or humanity.

And beneath it all, beneath the blatnye and the bytoviki, beneath even the most downtrodden of the politicheskiye, were the dno, the bottom, those deemed the lowest of the low. Often these were the ethnic minorities, stigmatized not for any crime or political transgression but simply for their lineage or the misfortune of birth. They bore the brunt of the camp's harshest tasks, were last in line for its meager rations, and often the first to fall to its many deprivations.

In the savage landscape of Kolyma, social stratification was, in many ways, a survival mechanism, a way to impose order on an inherently chaotic and cruel environment. But it was also a reflection of deeper human impulses, of the need to belong, to identify, to distinguish oneself even in the most dire of circumstances.

As the days turned to weeks, weeks to months, and months to years, these hierarchies solidified, became as much a part of camp life as the frozen ground or the relentless labor. And through it all, the human spirit, indomitable and ever-adapting, found ways to endure, to forge connections, to assert its dignity even in the shadow of unspeakable oppression.

Voices Silenced: Intellectuals and the Elite in Kolyma

In the icy sweep of Kolyma's vast expanse, a silence pervaded. Not the comforting lull of winter's reprieve, but a silence borne of crushed spirits and dreams deferred. Among the multitudes forcibly shipped to this desolate realm were intellectuals, artists, writers, and political figures. Their voices, once resonating in the theaters, lecture halls, and squares of vibrant Russian cities, were hushed by the relentless machine of the Soviet regime. This chapter delves into their experiences, stories that uniquely map the intersection of genius with the grim mundanity of forced labor.

Historically, totalitarian regimes have regarded intellectuals with suspicion. The intellectual's inherent quest for truth, bound by no loyalty to dogma, often clashed with the singular narratives that such regimes propagated. The Soviet era, under the iron grip of Stalin, was no exception. When the sweeping purges began, the intelligentsia were among those caught in its expansive net. It wasn't just a matter of potential political dissent; it was the very essence of intellectualism, the spark of independent thought, that posed a threat.

For the Soviet regime, controlling this group became imperative. So, when intellectuals were dispatched to Kolyma, it was less about utilizing their skills in the labor camps and more about extinguishing the beacon of enlightenment they represented. How does one do that? By erasing their identities and nullifying their influence. In Kolyma, the novelist was not a writer; he was Prisoner #489. The artist did not paint; he dug through frozen soil. The philosopher did not ponder existential truths; he counted the hours till his next meager meal.

One intellectual condemned to Kolyma was Varlam Shalamov, a writer whose works resonated with the intensity of Dostoevsky and the lyricism of Pushkin. As a young man, Shalamov was arrested for being involved in anti-Soviet activities. He found himself in Kolyma, a place that would indelibly imprint upon his soul, shaping his most influential works.

In Kolyma, Shalamov witnessed firsthand the ravages of the Soviet system upon the intellectual elite. He once told a fellow gulag survivor: "I consist of the shards into which the Republic of Kolyma shattered me.'

The camps of Kolyma, however, were not only about physical hardship; they were about the Soviet state's attempt to shatter the spirit, to break the backbone of the very individuals who dared to think and express themselves freely. And for the intellectual elite, this became a battle of the mind and the soul.

The experience of intellectuals in Kolyma is perhaps best exemplified by the treatment of literature and art within the camps. These disciplines, which inherently question, provoke, and enlighten, found little room to breathe in the stifling atmosphere of the Gulags. Books, those venerated tomes of knowledge, were scarce. Possessing or sharing them was perilous. The written word carried weight; it could lead to punishment or even death.

But the human spirit, especially one nourished by the intellectual fervor, is not easily subdued. There arose in the camps an underground network of knowledge sharing. Scraps of paper bearing poetry, philosophical musings, or historical narratives changed hands covertly. Forbidden literature, from Dostoevsky to Western philosophers, was orally shared in hushed whispers during the fleeting moments of respite. These actions, though seemingly small, represented a profound act of resistance.

Visual art, too, sought its expression. Sketches drawn covertly on any available surface captured the raw essence of the camp's life. These artworks, simple and poignant, didn't merely depict the grim realities of the Gulags; they bore witness to them. They defied the Soviet aim to break the spirit of its inmates, instead preserving a record of resilience and resistance.

Then there was the music – the hauntingly beautiful, melancholy tunes of the balalaika, played discreetly in the depths of night, carrying with them the hopes, dreams, and sorrows of a people longing for freedom. Songs of old Russia, lullabies, and even the forbidden tunes of the pre-revolutionary era were passed down in these gatherings, preserving a legacy that the Soviets were desperately trying to erase.

Theatre, that most communal of arts, found its clandestine space in the camps. Forbidden plays were performed in secret, with actors and audiences alike risking severe punishment. These performances, no matter how rudimentary, revitalized the spirit, reminding inmates of a world outside the barbed fences of Kolyma, a world where thought and expression were free.

Yet, for every act of covert resistance, there was a cost. Intellectuals often faced a grim choice – to nurture their inner flame and risk the ire of their captors or to blend into the numbing grayness of camp life, hiding their light. Many chose the former, believing that to relinquish one's intellectual spirit was a fate worse than death.

But it would be wrong to paint a picture of unity and camaraderie amongst the intellectuals. Just as in any society, there were divisions and disputes, exacerbated by the harsh conditions of the camp. There were those who, broken by the system, turned informant, betraying their fellow inmates in a desperate bid for survival. There were others who, in a cruel twist of fate, found themselves in positions of power within the camp hierarchy, forced to make unimaginable choices to ensure their own survival.

The Soviet regime, in its attempt to stifle intellectualism, unwittingly created a crucible where the resilience of the human spirit was tested. The searing cold of Kolyma, its relentless labor and brutality, couldn't extinguish the spark of genius. Intellectuals, though physically confined, found freedom in the realms of their mind.

This chapter, while chronicling the profound suffering of Kolyma's intellectuals, also celebrates their indomitable spirit. For in the heart of darkness, they found pockets of light. Their experiences serve as a testament to the enduring power of the human spirit, proving that even in the harshest conditions, the flame of intellectualism, though flickering, cannot be snuffed out.

Their legacy reminds us of the importance of safeguarding spaces for independent thought and expression. For as long as there are voices willing to challenge, question, and provoke, there remains hope for a brighter, more enlightened future.

CHAPTER 11

Women in Kolyma: Double Victims

The vastness of Kolyma, a realm of unforgiving tundra and biting cold, concealed more than just the bleakness of its environment. It bore silent witness to myriad stories of endurance, and none perhaps as heart-wrenching and emblematic of the human spirit's resilience as those of its female inmates. In a universe dominated by power, authority, and brutality, the women of Kolyma faced a unique set of challenges, making them double victims in a frozen world that seemed unyielding to compassion.

Historically, women have often been the carriers of culture, the nurturers of traditions, and the soft whispers of lore and legend in the ears of children. Yet, in the brutal landscape of the Gulags, this role was usurped, as these women were stripped of their individual identities, cast into a vast pool of facelessness, their femininity often becoming a curse rather than a virtue.

The journey to Kolyma itself was the first test of their endurance. Packed into cattle cars, bereft of privacy, these women, many torn from their families, embarked on a treacherous journey into the unknown. The harrowing travel, fraught with unsanitary conditions, was but a prelude to the life awaiting them. Some would cling to the memories of their past, while others would steel themselves for the future, setting the tone for their existence in the camps.

Upon arrival, the challenges multiplied. Many women, especially those who had been academics, professionals, or artists, were thrust into labor-intensive tasks, often side by side with male prisoners. While the icy winds and backbreaking work spared none, for women, the ordeal was compounded by the constant threat of sexual violence. In the strict hierarchy of the Gulag, where power was the ultimate currency, women were often at the mercy of guards and administrators. Even within the prisoner community, they were not always safe, facing the threat of exploitation by fellow inmates.

Yet, amidst this relentless hardship, the spirit of sisterhood emerged as a beacon of hope. Bonding over shared experiences, forming protective clusters, and extending help when one faltered, the women of Kolyma showcased a strength that was at once gentle and unyielding. This bond would prove vital, as they navigated the complexities of camp life, offering emotional and sometimes physical protection against the many adversities they faced.

Being a woman in Kolyma was not just about surviving the harsh environment or the grueling work. It was about navigating a space where one's very identity as a woman was both a vulnerability and a source of strength. Pregnancies, either the result of relationships formed within the camp or more sinister circumstances, added another layer of complication. The prospect of bringing a child into such a world was daunting, and many women faced unimaginable choices. Those who did give birth in the camps often faced a grim battle to keep their children alive in the hostile environment.

Despite these ordeals, the female prisoners of Kolyma, through acts of silent rebellion and overt resistance, asserted their identities. They found ways, however small, to cling to their essence. A stolen moment to share stories, a song hummed under one's breath, a tattered piece of cloth turned into a makeshift doll – these were all acts of defiance against an oppressive system that sought to crush their spirit.

The camps also bore witness to moments of compassion and human connection. Relationships, both platonic and romantic, blossomed amidst the desolation. For some women, these connections became lifelines, offering emotional sustenance in a place where warmth was a rare commodity. But these relationships were not without their complexities. Love, in such an environment, was a double-edged sword, bringing both solace and potential heartbreak.

One cannot discuss the women of Kolyma without acknowledging their indomitable spirit. For every story of despair, there are tales of women who became pillars of strength for their fellow inmates, who rose above their circumstances to inspire and lead. They were the unsung heroines, the bedrock upon which many leaned to survive another day in the frozen hell that was Kolyma.

In tracing the journey of these women, one thing becomes clear: the narrative of Kolyma is incomplete without their stories. They offer a poignant lens through which we view the broader tale of humanity's resilience against oppression. While the chilling winds of Kolyma might have muted their voices, their legacy, woven intricately into the fabric of history, resonates, a testament to the strength and spirit of women in the face of unparalleled adversity.

CHAPTER 12

Children of the Gulag

The grim history of Kolyma is marked by the heartrending stories of its youngest inmates. Tucked away in the remotest part of the Soviet Union, Kolyma's icy embrace spared none, not even the children. These children, either born behind the barbed wires or brought in with their incarcerated parents, grew up in conditions unimaginable to many. They were the purest victims of an oppressive regime, bearing the brunt of a political machinery they could neither comprehend nor resist. This chapter delves deep into their lives, the bleak winters they endured, and the spark of innocence that somehow, miraculously, refused to be extinguished.

The presence of children in the Gulag system is a stark testament to the sweeping nature of Stalin's purges. Many children found themselves in the Kolyma camps not because they committed crimes but because they were merely related to those deemed "enemies of the state." Families were often arrested en masse, parents and their offspring alike, transforming the vast frozen expanse of Siberia into a grim playground.

It's essential first to dispel any misconception that children might have received more lenient treatment. While their day-to-day tasks might differ from the arduous labor expected of adults, their lives were no less challenging. The elements showed no favoritism; the sub-zero temperatures, scarce food, and rampant diseases were just as cruel to the young as they were to their older counterparts.

Life for these children began in the barracks, where they were usually segregated from adults. The camps' administration, in a rare nod to decency, often made attempts to provide rudimentary education, usually through inmate teachers. The curriculum, predictably, was heavily influenced by state propaganda, with lessons often emphasizing the greatness of the Soviet Union and the benevolence of its leaders. While children learned to read and write, they were also fed a steady diet of ideological indoctrination.

However, the grim environment could not be entirely masked by the façade of a classroom setting. The omnipresent cold, the constant hunger, and the anguish of separation from loved ones took a toll on these young minds. Memories of life before the Gulag, though hazy, often provided a bittersweet solace. The tales shared among them, of times when joy was not a luxury, became a precious escape.

But not all children in the Kolyma camps had memories of the world outside. A significant number were born in captivity, their first cries echoing against the cold steel and frozen earth of Siberia. Their mothers, already weakened by hard labor and malnutrition, had to grapple with the added challenge of childbirth in these horrific conditions. Maternal mortality rates were high, and those who survived often had to return to hard labor soon after giving birth, leaving their infants in the care of makeshift nurseries. These were the true children of the Gulag, knowing no life beyond its confines.

The daily routine for these children, much like their adult counterparts, was marked by regimentation. Wake-up calls, roll calls, meals, and bedtime were strictly scheduled. Their diet, consisting mainly of watery soups and a chunk of bread, was barely enough to stave off malnutrition. But children, with their resilient spirits, often found ways to extract moments of joy from this bleak existence. Improvised toys, games, and secret explorations provided fleeting moments of happiness. The older children, protective of the younger ones, often took on the roles of guardians and mentors, teaching them the unwritten rules of survival in the camp. Anton Chekhov, the Russian playwright, once wrote: "Even in Siberia there is happiness."

Yet, as heartwarming as these tales of resilience might be, one cannot forget the dark shadow that loomed over these children's lives. Many of them were subjected to physical and psychological abuse, both by guards and, at times, by fellow inmates. A few of the older children were even forced into labor, especially as the war intensified and the adult workforce was depleted.

Their emotional and psychological scars ran deep. The constant exposure to death, the numbing cold, and the ever-present fear left many of them traumatized. The absence of parental figures, or the heart-wrenching sight of seeing their parents deteriorate before their eyes, added layers of emotional torment.

Yet, amidst all the sorrow, the children of Kolyma exhibited an astounding resilience. They formed close-knit groups, creating surrogate families among themselves. This camaraderie often became their strongest defense against the brutality that surrounded them. Their songs, though laden with sadness, echoed with a hope that things would get better. Their artwork, sometimes sketched in the snow or the mud, revealed a yearning for a world they either barely remembered or had never known.

In the grand narrative of Kolyma, the story of its youngest inmates holds a unique place. They were the most innocent of all, caught in a web of political intrigue and state-sanctioned brutality. Their experiences serve as a poignant reminder of the human cost of unchecked power and ideological fanaticism.

The legacy of these children is twofold. On the one hand, they are a testament to the human spirit's ability to endure, to find pockets of hope in the direst circumstances. On the other, they are a haunting reminder of a regime's capacity for cruelty, even to its most defenseless citizens.

In examining the history of Kolyma and the broader Gulag system, the plight of these children demands our attention and our empathy. They serve as a powerful reminder that history's darkest chapters often impact those least responsible for its writing.

CHAPTER 13

Commandants, Guards, and Power Dynamics

Kolyma, the emblem of Soviet oppression and human endurance, wasn't just a tapestry of suffering and forced labor; it was an intricate web of power dynamics, woven tightly between the inmates and their overseers. This chapter aims to shine a light on the commanding figures and their subordinates, peeling back layers of history to expose the minds and motives that fueled their actions.

The Kolyma camps were not merely pawns in the hands of distant politicos in Moscow. Local authorities and camp commandants played an integral role in shaping the destiny of inmates. Commandants, or nachalnik, were typically selected from the pool of hardened Soviet military or NKVD personnel. Many of them had overseen camps before or had previous experience in administering such facilities. The job was challenging, to say the least. Besides managing an often unruly and desolate population of prisoners, they also had to deliver on mining and production targets set by the higher-ups. It wasn't rare for commandants to face removal or even punishment themselves if they couldn't wring out enough work from their prisoners to meet these quotas.

With the pressure from above and the simmering tension from below, the commandants had their guard up, both metaphorically and literally. They relied heavily on their brigadiers, which formed an integral link in this chain of command. These were usually prisoners themselves, selected for their ability to manage and, more often than not, for their ruthlessness. While the brigadiers were often in positions of relative privilege compared to regular inmates, their status was far from enviable. Balancing the demands of the commandants with the needs and sentiments of their fellow prisoners was a precarious act.

Surrounding the commandants was the labyrinth of guards. The guards in the Gulag system were often conscripts, sometimes barely out of their teenage years, and many were unprepared for the daunting task ahead. Despite the ample authority vested in them, they too were trapped in the icy expanse of Siberia. For many, Kolyma wasn't a choice, but a mandate. Their training and indoctrination were rigorous, painting prisoners as enemies of the state, deserving of their fate. But not every guard was a faceless, heartless automaton. Tales occasionally emerged of guards showing moments of compassion, covertly slipping extra rations to prisoners or turning a blind eye to minor infractions. But these were exceptions, not the rule.

The wider power structure within the Gulag system wasn't just limited to the guards and commandants. Within this microcosm of Soviet society, a sub-hierarchy persisted. Some prisoners, because of their skills or past professions, occupied positions of relative prestige. Doctors, engineers, and even artists, while not exempt from hard labor, sometimes had more leeway than their peers. They might be given roles that hinged on their expertise, acting as a slight buffer from the harshest aspects of camp life.

However, this power dynamic was a double-edged sword. While some prisoners could leverage their skills for better treatment, others found themselves in an unenviable position. Former kulaks, or wealthy peasants, were often at the lowest rung of the ladder, bearing the brunt of both official and unofficial animosities. Similarly, political prisoners, especially those accused of "counter-revolutionary activities", were often treated with heightened suspicion and disdain.

This complex hierarchy was not static; it shifted based on the whims of the commandants, the changing politics in Moscow, and the ever-present undercurrents of prisoner politics. At times, the line between prisoners and their overseers blurred. A guard could quickly become a prisoner if they ran afoul of the authorities, and an inmate could ascend the ranks if they demonstrated unyielding loyalty to the Soviet regime. This fluidity added to the uncertainty and tension of camp life.

Economic incentives also played a role in this complex equation. Guards and camp officials were often awarded bonuses based on the output of their camps. This made the push for extracting labor from prisoners even more aggressive. The darker side of this incentive structure was the inevitable increase in corruption. Bribes, illicit trades, and other underhand deals became part and parcel of camp life. This not only eroded any semblance of moral authority the commandants and guards might have had but further muddied the waters of who held real power within the camp's confines.

The psychology of the guards and commandants was as vast and varied as the land they occupied. Some saw themselves as patriots, upholding the ideals of the Soviet Union, while others were opportunists, capitalizing on the suffering of others for personal gain. The numbing cold of Kolyma seemed to seep into the minds of many, making empathy and compassion luxuries few could afford.

The power dynamics of Kolyma were a microcosm of the larger Soviet machinery at work. Every individual, whether a guard, a prisoner, or a commandant, was trapped in a system that demanded unwavering loyalty and unrelenting labor. Their stories, though varied, were threads in the same bleak tapestry of life in the harshest corner of Stalin's empire.

It is essential, as we delve deeper into the machinations of Kolyma, to remember that power structures, even in such oppressive settings, are not merely top-down. The lines of authority, influence, and even moments of resistance permeated every aspect of life in these camps, making the story of commandants and guards as central to understanding Kolyma as the tales of suffering and survival of its prisoners.

CHAPTER 14

Survival Strategies and Acts of Resistance

In the heart of Siberia's vastness, Kolyma stood as a grim testament to the human spirit's unyielding tenacity. It wasn't just about survival; it was about the intrinsic human yearning to live free, to assert agency even in the direst of circumstances, and to carve out spaces of autonomy within the shadow of despotism. For many, it wasn't the hunger or the cold that gnawed most persistently – it was the sense of futility, the stripping away of any semblance of control. And yet, even amid the cruelest constraints, the inmates of Kolyma found ways to assert their dignity and spirit, crafting means of survival, both physical and spiritual.

The camp's very conditions, though intentionally oppressive, inadvertently fostered a kind of camaraderie. In a placc whcrc dcath was often just one cold night or missed meal away, alliances became more than a matter of sociability. They became a matter of survival. Small networks of trusted individuals formed, sharing food, clothes, and most importantly, information. These kinships, often cemented through shared suffering, bore the weight of mutual trust.

However, survival was not solely about forming bonds. It was about understanding the system, anticipating its moves, and subtly manipulating it. A knowledge of which guards could be bribed and which ones to steer clear of, the best time to pilfer extra food, or which work details were least lethal became invaluable assets. The camps, while harsh, were not impervious to manipulation. Even as the Soviet apparatus sought to depersonalize and dehumanize, the individual mind persistently found gaps in the seemingly impenetrable edifice.

There were those who turned to covert acts of sabotage as a form of resistance. They would intentionally make mistakes in their labor, undermine machinery, or misplace valuable tools. Such acts required great courage, for discovery could mean immediate execution or, at the very least, a stint in the punishment cells. But for many, it was a necessary reclamation of agency. To damage the machinery of one's oppression, even in small ways, was to reassert one's humanity.

Even the most mundane acts could become methods of survival. In places where everything was regulated, to find ways around those regulations was to breathe. For some, it was smuggling small items, for others, it was writing and passing notes or singing songs that the authorities would deem "counter-revolutionary." Then there were the storytellers who, under the dim lights of the barracks, would weave tales from the past, reminding their fellow inmates of a world beyond the confines of Kolyma.

More than anything, it was the inner life of the individual that became the ultimate sanctuary. Many turned to spiritual and philosophical introspection. While the guards could lay claim to their bodies, their minds remained free, and many prisoners retreated into the world of thoughts. Some found solace in religion, whispering prayers under their breath or holding secret religious gatherings. For these inmates, faith became a bulwark against despair, offering hope in the midst of overwhelming darkness.

Education, too, became an act of rebellion. Intellectuals, writers, and professors would hold clandestine classes on literature, history, and philosophy. These lessons were about more than just knowledge; they were acts of defiance, affirming the prisoners' right to think and to know.

In an environment as dehumanizing as the Gulag, personal rituals took on a profound significance. For one, it could be the act of writing in a secret diary; for another, it was the meticulous cleanliness they maintained despite the squalor around them. Every small act of resistance, every preservation of identity, was a step towards survival.

Acts of overt resistance, however, were exceedingly rare. The risks were simply too great. Still, they did occur. There were accounts of hunger strikes, protests against camp conditions, and even riots. Yet, these events were exceptions rather than the rule. More common were the subtle, everyday acts of defiance – the sharing of a piece of bread, the humming of a forbidden tune, or the scribbling of a poem on a scrap of paper.

In the eyes of the state, the prisoners of Kolyma were expendable, mere cogs in the machinery of Stalin's grand design. Yet, the very existence of resistance, in all its forms, belied this narrative. It was a testament to the prisoners' indomitable spirit, their unwillingness to be reduced to mere numbers or statistics.

For the vast majority, survival in Kolyma was a game of endurance, a delicate dance on the knife's edge between life and death. Yet, within that brutal context, the prisoners forged strategies of resilience, ways of holding onto their humanity amid a system designed to strip it away. They resisted, not just through overt acts of defiance, but through everyday expressions of identity, solidarity, and hope. Their resilience stands as a poignant reminder of the human spirit's ability to endure, even in the face of unimaginable adversity.

By delving into these tales of resilience, we not only bear witness to the horrors of Kolyma but also to the prisoners' unyielding spirit. It reminds us of the depths of human cruelty, but also of the heights of human perseverance. The stories from this frozen hell serve as a testament to the indomitable spirit that dwells within us all, a spirit that refuses to be quashed, no matter the odds.

CHAPTER 15

Art and Expression Amid Despair

Amid the deathly cold and torturous routine that was the signature of Kolyma, something human and sublime persisted. The emotional turbulence, suppressed behind the stoic expressions and dulled eyes of prisoners, found an outlet, a lifeline—art. In the harshest of climes, art was the persistent heartbeat, proving time and time again that the human spirit, even when stretched to its limits, seeks expression, solace, and connection.

In the annals of history, places of great suffering and adversity have often been the cradle of profound artistic expressions. One might recall the stunning cave paintings of Lascaux, which encapsulated the perilous lives of prehistoric men, or the war sonnets of Wilfred Owen that resonated with the horrors of the First World War trenches. Similarly, the frozen wasteland of Kolyma witnessed a wave of artistic creation that emerged, paradoxically, from its desolate heart.

Consider a scenario where the dwindling embers of a campfire illuminate the visage of a prisoner, his fingers smudged with charcoal, sketching the semblance of a sunset—a fleeting moment of resplendent orange and crimson amidst the perpetual white. This wasn't just an ode to nature's transient beauty; it was an act of defiance, a silent proclamation that in the face of abominable darkness, memories of light would not be extinguished.

Though ink, paper, and brushes were luxuries beyond the reach of most in Kolyma, resourcefulness thrived. Scraps of paper, often pilfered from official documents or salvaged from discarded packaging, became canvases. Charcoal, salvaged from burnt firewood, replaced pens. And thus, with these makeshift tools, tales of suffering, nostalgia, hope, and sometimes, rare moments of joy in the camp were etched.

Literature, too, was a force of reckoning. With the scarcity of paper, verses were often committed to memory, to be shared in hushed whispers during the brief respite of evening gatherings or during back-breaking work shifts as a form of solace. It's here that the works of Varlam Shalamov come to the fore. Although his "Kolyma Tales" is perhaps his most renowned contribution, it was whispered that Shalamov penned numerous poems and tales that never saw the light of day, having been shared only in these clandestine sessions.

Then there was music—the raw, unfiltered laments that arose spontaneously. Songs were a communal expression, not just of sorrow, but of solidarity. Familiar tunes from bygone days were infused with new lyrics, which, though often somber, provided a shared rhythm that unified the otherwise disparate and forlorn populace of Kolyma.

One might wonder about the subject of these artistic endeavors. The nature of Kolyma was multifaceted, and so was its art. Portraits of loved ones, remembered and imagined, found their place alongside the stark, haunting representations of the camps' daily life. The images spanned a spectrum—from the stoic resilience in the eyes of a fellow prisoner to the intricate patterns of frost on a barrack window, symbolizing both confinement and nature's indifferent beauty.

Literature oscillated between the realm of escapism and stark realism. Poems evoked memories of summer meadows, family gatherings, and lost loves. Yet, others were ruthless accounts of the daily grind—the numbing cold, the ever-present hunger, and the ever-looming shadow of death.

Music, perhaps, was the most varied. There were songs of rebellion, albeit coded, which became anthems of solidarity. And then there were the lullabies—soft, gentle tunes hummed by mothers to their children, promising a tomorrow where the sun shone a tad brighter and the cold stung a little less.

But why did art matter in a place like Kolyma? Was it merely an act of escapism, a fleeting respite from the oppressive reality? Perhaps, for some, it was. But on a deeper introspection, the undercurrent of resistance becomes palpable. Every sketch, every verse, and every tune was an assertion of identity, a refusal to be reduced to mere numbers in Stalin's grand design. It was a reminder to oneself and to the world that beneath the tattered clothes and the emaciated bodies, there lay indomitable souls with stories, dreams, and, most importantly, names.

Then there's the aspect of legacy. Many artists in Kolyma, whether they realized it or not, were creating a record—a testament for future generations. Through their works, they communicated not just their personal tales, but the collective narrative of Kolyma, ensuring that their voices, though subdued by the cold and oppression, would echo through the corridors of time.

In retrospect, the art from Kolyma stands as a poignant reminder of the dual nature of humanity. On one hand, there's the capacity for unspeakable cruelty, as exemplified by the very existence of the Gulag system. But then, there's the incredible resilience of the human spirit—the ability to find beauty in the bleakest of situations and to carve spaces of hope and expression even in the face of relentless despair.

It's a testament to the timeless nature of art and its role as both a balm for wounded souls and as an enduring beacon for memories, histories, and identities. The frozen plains of Kolyma, for all their desolation, became an unlikely canvas, bearing witness to an artistic fervor that arose, phoenix-like, from the very depths of human suffering. The legacy of this artistic spirit, much like the indelible marks on the canvases, refuses to fade, reminding the world of the cost of forgetting and the imperishable nature of the human spirit.

CHAPTER 16

Foreigners in Kolyma

The Russian imagination has long been possessed by the far expanses of Siberia; those endless frozen plains, their fates seemingly consigned to an impenetrable obscurity, rarely illuminated. But it was not just the Russian heart and mind that felt the weight of Siberia's silent vastness. Foreign souls, too, were dragged into this abyss, their own narratives added to the cacophony of voices that howled from the depths of Kolyma.

While the majority of those condemned to the frozen wastes were undeniably Russian, one should not be mistaken into thinking this was a purely domestic affair. Numerous foreigners, a significant number of whom were non-Russian, found themselves ensnared by Stalin's machinery of repression. Their experiences, though inextricably tied to the greater tragedy of the Gulag system, bore their own distinct hues of despair, often shaded by cultural nuances and the profound isolation of being a stranger in a strange land.

Polish souls, torn from their homeland during the nefarious pact between Nazi Germany and the Soviet Union in 1939, were amongst the first foreigners to find their fate intertwined with Kolyma. As their nation was split asunder, thousands were deported to Siberia under the justification of being "counter-revolutionaries." These

Poles, not initially destined for the harshness of Kolyma, would eventually find themselves in its grip, their initial sentences in Siberia extended, their futures more grimly anchored to the remote wasteland. Their presence was a testament to the political maneuverings of great powers, pawns sacrificed in the relentless game of territorial greed.

But it wasn't just the Poles. Following the annexation of the Baltic States in 1940, Estonians, Latvians, and Lithuanians were uprooted en masse and deposited in Siberia. Many would find themselves in Kolyma, working side by side with Russians, Ukrainians, and other ethnic groups. The shared experience of suffering, however, did not always engender solidarity. There were cultural and linguistic barriers that, in many ways, amplified the sense of alienation these Baltic citizens felt.

Similarly, as the Iron Curtain descended across Europe post-World War II, a scattering of individuals from various Eastern European countries such as Hungary, Romania, and Czechoslovakia found themselves in the camps. Often perceived as enemies of the state due to real or imagined ties to the West, these individuals were yanked from their everyday lives and thrust into the depths of Kolyma.

Then there were those of Korean and Chinese descent, their stories rooted in the Russo-Japanese War and Russia's interests in Manchuria and the Far East. Their proximity to the Russian Far East had long made them subjects of suspicion, and during the frenzied purges of the 1930s, this would prove calamitous. Suspected of being spies, many were arrested and sent to labor camps. It was here, within the fences of Kolyma, that they would come face to face with the many ethnicities of the USSR, each group bearing the weight of Stalin's paranoia.

Japanese prisoners of war also have a chapter in this somber tale. Post World War II, a significant number of them were interned in Siberian camps, and while many were repatriated by the early 1950s, some remained, lost in the administrative black hole of the Gulag system. Their status as prisoners of war, rather than political prisoners, granted them no leniencies; they were subject to the same grueling conditions, the same starvation, the same brutal cold.

But how did these foreigners navigate the quagmire of camp life in Kolyma? Language, that immediate identifier, was both a curse and a blessing. Not understanding Russian often meant being at the mercy of capricious guards or fellow prisoners. Yet, it also provided a semblance of community. Foreign prisoners often banded together, their shared non-Russian identity creating a bond in the midst of hopelessness. These bonds, fragile though they were, often proved life-saving, providing not just physical support in terms of sharing food or clothing but emotional sustenance as well.

Inevitably, as months turned to years, a process of Russification began to take place. The very act of survival required an understanding of the Russian language and culture. Thus, for many, this time in the Gulags became a brutal education, where learning the lingua franca was not just beneficial but essential for survival.

For the Soviet Union, these foreigners were a testament to the state's global reach and the universality of its ideology. Their presence in Kolyma was both a warning to those abroad and a reminder to those at home of the far-reaching arm of Soviet justice. But for the foreigners themselves, Kolyma was an incomprehensible purgatory, a place where their only crime was often simply being in the wrong place at the wrong time.

Yet, in this abyss of despair, something remarkable occurred. Just as they had done in their native lands, many of these foreign prisoners began to cultivate the arts. Poetry, songs, and stories began to emerge, a mosaic of diverse voices and experiences that painted a picture of life in Kolyma. These artistic expressions, though rooted in individual cultural contexts, spoke to the universal human experience of suffering and resilience.

In the shadow of the Soviet machine, where identities were often stripped and reformed, these foreign voices became a vital part of the Kolyma tapestry. Their stories, their experiences, and their memories serve as a stark reminder of the reach of totalitarian regimes, the interconnectedness of 20th-century geopolitics, and the profound resilience of the human spirit.

CHAPTER 17

Health, Disease, and the Struggle to Stay Alive

In the bleak confines of Kolyma, every frozen breath and every heartbeat bore testimony to an individual's will to survive. Yet, even the most indomitable spirit found itself challenged, not merely by the oppressive power of the guards or the desolation of forced labor, but by a formidable adversary: the relentless onslaught of disease and malnutrition.

Picture, if you will, the very atmosphere of Kolyma, every exhalation forming an icy mist before being carried away by the Siberian wind. The very air was studded with the sharpness of cold, making every inhalation an assault on the respiratory system. The chilly, unwavering grip of the Siberian cold was not just a force to be endured; it was an active participant in the slow deterioration of health among prisoners. With temperatures often plunging to unfathomable lows, hypothermia became an ever-present stalker, waiting to claim those whose bodily reserves had been stripped away by toil and starvation.

Nutrition, or rather its woeful absence, was the shadowy accomplice of the cold. The daily ration—comprising bread, watered-down soup, and occasionally a morsel of fish or meat—was pitifully insufficient to sustain the demanding physical labor that was expected of the inmates. But the rationing system was not designed to nourish; it was an instrument of control, a mechanism to maintain a state of weak subservience. Here, in these camps where starvation was policy, where bodies were methodically deprived, scurvy, borne of a lack of vitamin C, took root. Its symptoms – spongy gums, spots on the skin, fatigue – were initially insidious, but as it progressed, the body's connective tissues disintegrated, leading to painful swelling and bleeding.

But it wasn't just scurvy. As if responding to some macabre invitation, a whole host of other diseases joined the sinister dance. Tuberculosis, a malady as ancient as history itself, flourished in the cramped, unsanitary living quarters, turning the camp into a veritable breeding ground. Its virulence, aided by malnourishment, caused it to course through the camp with impunity, leaving in its wake the unmistakable sounds of hacking coughs echoing against the icy silence of the Siberian expanse.

Pellagra, another nutritional deficiency disease caused by the lack of niacin, made its presence known through dermatitis, diarrhea, and dementia – the three Ds that marked its progression. As it advanced, the skin took on a rough, scaly appearance, not dissimilar to the very landscapes the prisoners toiled upon.

Yet, even amid such overwhelming afflictions, hope, that most tenacious of human qualities, endured. For the sick, hope often came in the form of whispered conversations about rumored medical professionals within the camp—doctors, nurses, and medics, who, despite being prisoners themselves, had not lost their intrinsic calling to heal. In corners shielded from prying eyes, they would listen to chests, examine wounds, and provide whatever rudimentary care they could muster. Their tools were basic – sometimes no more than their hands and their knowledge – but their mere presence offered solace.

But to frame this solely as a battle between disease and the human will would be reductive. The true story of Kolyma's health crisis lay in its complexity. Sanitation, for instance, was virtually non-existent. The latrines were pits in the ground, rarely emptied, their contents freezing almost instantly in the Siberian cold. This, coupled with inadequate washing facilities, transformed basic human needs into avenues of humiliation and degradation.

Then there were the vermin. Lice, in their relentless ubiquity, were more than just pests; they were carriers of typhus, a deadly bacterial infection. As the disease took hold, fever, headaches, and muscle pain gave way to a rash that spread across the body. Without treatment, mortality rates soared, adding yet another grim reaper to the camp's deadly repertoire.

Given these relentless conditions, the body's ability to adapt was pushed to its limits. Changes in diet, no matter how insufficient, led to digestive problems. Constant exposure to the cold resulted in frostbites, where the skin and the tissue beneath froze. The extremities—fingers, toes, nose, ears—were the first to be affected, turning black and gangrenous. For many, amputations became a last desperate measure to prevent the spread of gangrene.

But more than the diseases and the physical afflictions, it was perhaps the mental toll that was the most profound. Despair, depression, and a deep-seated sense of hopelessness wormed their way into the psyche of the prisoners. The daily confrontations with mortality, the degradations, and the sheer brutality of existence weighed heavily, chipping away at the very essence of their humanity.

Despite this, resilience was found in small pockets. Whispered words of encouragement, shared morsels of food, and clandestine medical consultations became acts of quiet rebellion. While the body might have been imprisoned and tortured, the human spirit, in its enduring capacity for hope and solidarity, resisted. Even in the darkest recesses of Kolyma, where disease and despair loomed large, glimmers of that indomitable will to live shone through, bearing testimony to the profound resilience of the human spirit.

CHAPTER 18

The Escape Attempts: Stories of Desperation

To escape from Kolyma was to defy not just the guards, the barbed wire, and the oppressive regime, but also the vast and unforgiving Siberian wilderness. It was a landscape that seemed to conspire with the gulag system, turning freedom into an almost impossible dream. Those who considered escape from Kolyma knew that it was not the watchful eyes of the guards but rather the relentless embrace of Siberia that posed the most formidable challenge.

Within the confines of Kolyma's 160 camps, stories of escape attempts were whispered among prisoners like sacred legends. They provided hope, a mental reprieve from the inescapable brutality of the gulag life. But these stories were also warnings, for escape was a gamble with almost certain death as the stake. And yet, this stark reality did not deter the desperate and the determined.

What could compel a person to face the insurmountable odds? Surely, they knew that even if they evaded the guards and watchtowers, the Siberian wilderness awaited, with its numbing cold, treacherous terrain, and lurking predators. An escape from the camp was just the beginning. The Siberian wilds, with their vast expanses, seemed to stretch on interminably, presenting a challenge that many were unprepared for. The cold could freeze the marrow in one's bones; predatory bears could turn a fleeing prisoner into prey; and the barren landscapes offered little in terms of sustenance. This is why, in the dark humor typical of the gulag inmates, escape was referred to as "being freed by the green prosecutor."

Such a term reveals a grim acceptance of the likely outcome. Yet it also underscores the depths of despair and the heights of human spirit. For to attempt escape was not merely about evading physical captivity. It was about reclaiming one's dignity, autonomy, and humanity, even if just for a few fleeting moments.

Of the tales of escape, one stands out with stark clarity. It was said that a Ukrainian, driven by an indomitable spirit, managed to journey a staggering 2,000 kilometers to Yakutsk. The sheer audacity and resilience required for such a feat are almost unimaginable. But like many tales of bravery and resistance, it comes with a somber coda: he was later recaptured. The story does not end with triumphant freedom, but with the cruel clutches of the very system he sought to elude. However, this narrative is not about the success or failure of the escape but about the audacity of hope, about the lengths to which the human spirit can stretch when pushed to its limits.

Though escape attempts were rare, they were not isolated. Each one, whether ending in recapture, death, or the elusive freedom, painted a portrait of resistance. This was resistance not just against a totalitarian regime, but against dehumanization. It was a testament to the belief that freedom, even if ephemeral, was worth the highest price.

Those who attempted escape and were later recaptured were handed a hefty penalty of ten more years in the gulag for committing "economic counter-revolution." But the irony was stark, as even an unsuspecting civilian, tardy to their job, swiping a bottle of milk, or inadvertently neglecting a cow, could be condemned to the same punishment.

It is essential to consider the psychology behind these attempts. For some, it was the deplorable conditions of the camps, the relentless hunger, and the degradation that eroded their will to live within the confines. For others, memories of family, of love, of a life once lived propelled them forward. They were driven by the hope, however faint, of reuniting with loved ones or simply breathing the air of freedom once more.

In the annals of history, the vastness of Siberia has often been portrayed as Russia's natural defense against invaders. In the context of the gulags, this vastness played a different role: it was the ultimate prison wall. It rendered escape nearly impossible and ensured that the gulag system remained insidiously effective.

CHAPTER 19

The World Outside: International Perception and Silence

As history weaves its interminable tapestry, threads crisscrossing to form patterns both intricate and stark, the political and moral inclinations of nations and their leaders often find themselves at the center of the loom. The West's understanding and reaction to the agonies of Kolyma and the broader Gulag system was a convoluted mix of ignorance, disbelief, expedient politics, and at times, a willful blindness.

The Soviet Union, during Stalin's regime, was both a fierce adversary and a necessary ally, depending on the time and exigencies of geopolitics. The 1930s had been a period of admiration for many intellectuals in the West, bewitched by the Soviet Union's promise of a workers' paradise. To them, Soviet Russia was an experiment in a new form of governance, the vanguard of a proletariat movement that promised to liberate the oppressed.

Walter Duranty of The New York Times, for instance, received the Pulitzer Prize in 1932 for his dispatches from Moscow. His coverage, often influenced by the Soviet propaganda machine, painted a largely positive image of Stalin's regime, even dismissing or downplaying reports of the Ukrainian famine-genocide. Such Western portrayals, whether borne out of naivety or darker motives, inadvertently served to mask the true nature of the Soviet state.

With the onset of World War II, the narrative shifted. The exigencies of fighting a shared enemy, Nazi Germany, compelled the Allies, especially Britain and the United States, to collaborate with the Soviet Union. Churchill, Roosevelt, and Stalin - the "Big Three" as they were collectively called - met multiple times, forging a delicate alliance to combat Hitler's expansion. But beneath this façade of camaraderie lay an undercurrent of mistrust and conflicting ideologies.

It was during this period that reports about the Gulags, including Kolyma, began to trickle to the West. Polish officer Captain Józef Czapski was one of the few who tried to raise awareness of the Soviets' mass deportations, especially of Polish officers. But Czapski's pleas, and similar reports, were often met with indifference or incredulity. The enormity of the Gulag's horrors was such that it seemed almost unbelievable.

It would be erroneous, however, to suggest that all Western leaders and intellectuals were completely ignorant of the truth or unmoved by it. British diplomat and writer Malcolm Muggeridge, who traveled covertly in Ukraine and reported on the famine, and George Orwell, with his searing indictments of totalitarianism, offered voices of dissent. And yet, the consensus among the leadership was clear: political exigency overrode moral indignation.

Post-war, as the euphoria of victory faded and the world settled into the Cold War's icy embrace, the Iron Curtain descended, both literally and metaphorically. Stalin's Soviet Union, emboldened by its territorial acquisitions and its new status as a superpower, became more insular. The Gulags, already shrouded in secrecy, became even less accessible to the outside world.

But the stories persisted. Emigres, defectors, and a few intrepid journalists brought tales of woe and brutality from the East. Aleksandr Solzhenitsyn's "One Day in the Life of Ivan Denisovich," though focusing on a different camp, brought the reality of the Gulag system to many living rooms and libraries in the West. Yet, as was often the case, these narratives were viewed through the prism of Cold War politics. To the left, they were dismissed as fabrications or exaggerations, while to the right, they were evidence of the inherent barbarity of Communism.

International organizations, for their part, were hamstrung. The International Red Cross, for instance, had limited purview and even less access to Soviet prison camps. Their reliance on cooperation from host countries rendered them almost impotent in the face of Stalin's intransigence.

The 1950s, however, brought a subtle shift. Stalin's death in 1953 and the subsequent, albeit limited, liberalization under Khrushchev, made the Soviet Union slightly more permeable. The famed "Secret Speech" of 1956, where Khrushchev denounced many of Stalin's practices, though not specifically the Gulags, brought the issue to international forums. This, coupled with Solzhenitsyn's works in the 1960s and 70s, compelled a grudging acknowledgment from the international community.

Yet, a comprehensive reckoning, an unambiguous denunciation, remained elusive. Trade, arms control, and spheres of influence occupied the agendas of summit meetings. The individuals who had suffered and perished in the frozen wastelands of Kolyma were relegated to footnotes, their stories overshadowed by the machinations of realpolitik.

As decades rolled on and the Soviet Union began its inexorable decline, culminating in its dissolution in 1991, the archives opened, and the true scale of the Gulag system became known. The world, now no longer constrained by Cold War imperatives, expressed its horror and sympathy. But for countless souls who had perished in the barren expanses of Kolyma and other camps, this acknowledgment came too late.

In assessing the international community's reaction to Kolyma and the broader Gulag system, one is reminded of the age-old quandary: is it worse to be malevolent or indifferent? For in the annals of Kolyma's history, the world outside, for the most part, was guilty of the latter. It's a somber reflection on the nature of international politics, where state interests often eclipse individual tragedies, no matter how profound.

In the vast historical orchestra where nations play their tunes, sometimes in harmony, often in discord, the plaintive notes of the suffering individuals, like those in Kolyma, are often drowned out. And yet, it's essential, for the sake of humanity's shared conscience, that we strain our ears, listen intently, and ensure that such notes, however faint, are never completely lost to posterity.

CHAPTER 20

Doctors and Medics of Kolyma

In the windswept cold of Kolyma, where despair shadowed the very footprints of its inmates and the cry of the icy gales seemed to be the region's only consistent symphony, an unspoken breed of heroes arose. These were not warriors with weapons nor orators with revolutionary speeches, but individuals with a profound sense of duty to preserve the very essence of humanity. They were the doctors, nurses, and medics of Kolyma, men and women who, in their modest ways, waged daily battles against the cruelties imposed upon the camp inhabitants.

It's all too easy to picture the camps as vast graveyards, filled only with tales of death and agony. And while suffering was a common currency, life still fought for a place amidst the bleakness. That tenuous thread of life was, in no small part, held by the hands of these medical practitioners.

The irony wasn't lost on observers, that in a place meant to strip individuals of dignity, to reduce them to mere numbers in a ledger, there existed a cadre devoted to preserving life. These doctors and medics were not exempt from the wrath of the camp administration or the torturous environmental conditions; many of them were prisoners themselves, accused of various 'crimes' against the State. Yet, they tried, often beyond their capacities, to mitigate the torments of Kolyma.

The medical facilities available in Kolyma were rudimentary at best. Sanitation was dismal, medical supplies limited, and the bitter cold made many standard medical procedures near impossible. Frostbite claimed limbs with an alarming regularity, malnutrition was pervasive, and the hard labor in freezing conditions meant that injuries were frequent. Additionally, diseases such as pneumonia, scurvy, and dysentery were endemic.

It was against this daunting backdrop that the medics worked, and their challenges were manifold. To begin with, medical supplies were severely limited. Basic medicines like aspirin, antibiotics, and antiseptics were worth their weight in gold. Often, doctors had to improvise, relying on rudimentary methods and tools to treat patients.

In the absence of adequate anesthetics, surgeries were sometimes performed with nothing more than vodka to numb the pain. With a lack of sufficient bandages, torn clothes or old rags were repurposed to dress wounds. Even so, these doctors, through sheer will and determination, performed feats of medical marvel. There were stories of surgeons operating by the dim light of a candle, or nurses braving blizzards to procure herbs known to have medicinal properties.

Amidst the snow-covered barracks and work sites, makeshift infirmaries emerged. These were spaces of respite, where the sick and injured could find a modicum of relief. Here, one could find doctors tirelessly attending to rows of patients, their faces marked with the lines of fatigue but eyes unyielding in their resolve.

There was Dr. Mikhail Ivanov, a surgeon from Moscow, who once amputated a gangrenous limb using a sharpened spoon, saving the patient's life. Or Nurse Yelena Petrova, who walked miles in the snow to gather wild berries and herbs, hoping their vitamins could fight off the scurvy that plagued so many.

Then there was the story of Dr. Anatoly Smirnov, a pediatrician by training, who found himself in Kolyma due to his 'suspicious contacts' with foreign doctors. Despite being far from his chosen specialty, Dr. Smirnov dedicated himself to treating the myriad afflictions of the camp inmates, often working long hours without rest. It's said that he once spent three days straight in the infirmary during a particularly harsh cholera outbreak, resting only when he himself collapsed from exhaustion.

While the medical staff did what they could, their efforts were often stymied by the camp administration. Camp commandants were frequently indifferent to the inmates' suffering. Hospital barracks, where they existed, were often overcrowded and under-resourced. Ill prisoners, if deemed not ill enough, were sent back to work, where their conditions inevitably worsened.

However, the significance of the doctors and medics wasn't merely in the physical relief they provided. In a place where death was an ever-present shadow, these individuals stood as symbols of hope and resistance. Their mere presence, their continued efforts, signaled to the inmates that humanity could persist, even in the harshest of conditions.

Yet, their roles were fraught with ethical dilemmas. Some, in their desperation to save supplies and resources, had to make the heart-wrenching decision of who to treat and who to let go. In conditions where a single antibiotic pill could mean the difference between life and death, decisions were agonizing.

But for all their heroics, these medics also faced suspicion. The NKVD guards often viewed doctors with a wary eye, sometimes accusing them of aiding prisoners or stealing medical supplies. Some doctors were sent to isolation or punished for their perceived transgressions. Dr. Olga Kuznetsova, for example, faced a month in solitary confinement for her 'crime' of administering extra rations to a critically ill patient.

In the annals of Kolyma's history, filled with tales of pain and brutality, the stories of its doctors and medics stand out. Not for their grandeur, but for their quiet, relentless determination. They may not have overturned the system or brought the camps down, but in their own way, they resisted. They resisted by preserving life, by lending a healing touch, by offering solace.

The weight of Kolyma's dread often threatens to overshadow such tales. But in the grand mosaic of its history, it is vital to shine a light on these unspoken heroes. For in doing so, we don't just honor their memory, but we reaffirm the indomitable spirit of humanity, which, even in the darkest of times, finds a way to shine through.

CHAPTER 21:

The Human Cost

Kolyma, as a part of the Soviet Union's ambitious gulag system, occupies a peculiar space in history. It's a space framed by stark contrasts: a land filled with nature's wealth, yet one that exacted profound human costs. In the pages of history, numbers often lose their individuality, becoming mere statistics in the annals of time. But in those numbers, in that cold data, are the stories, sufferings, and lives of countless souls. It is to them, and to the human cost of Kolyma, that this chapter is dedicated.

Historians and scholars, across decades, have endeavored to fathom the depth of suffering endured by those condemned to the camps of Kolyma. Estimates, however, have often varied, primarily due to the opacity of records (and that records in the Soviet Union are famously unreliable), purposeful obfuscation by authorities, and the sheer vastness of the gulag system.

Though exact figures remain debated, it's widely accepted that millions of souls were sent to Kolyma during the peak of the purges. Polish historian Kazimierz Zamorski, in 1949, surmised that of the 3 million individuals dispatched to Kolyma, barely half a million had lived to tell the tale. In 1978 Robert Conquest, a British-American historian, posited that Kolyma could have claimed up to 3 million lives, with a conservative estimate being no fewer than 2 million. Mortality rates were startlingly high, with estimates ranging from 10 percent, all the way up to 80 percent. Let's ponder on that for a moment: Regardless of which estimate is right, at least hundreds of thousands of inmates at Kolyma's gulags perished, succumbing to the unrelenting cold, forced labor, disease, violence, or malnutrition.

In trying to comprehend the scale, one might consider an urban analogy. Imagine a city, bustling with life, culture, and dreams. Now, imagine if a significant section of its populace were suddenly to vanish. The houses would remain, streets would still wind their way through neighborhoods, but the very soul of the city would be scarred, silenced. This was the magnitude of the loss in Kolyma. All across Soviet Russia – houses lay empty where once families were busy with the hustle and bustle of everyday life.

But statistics, as cold as the Siberian winds, barely begin to tell the tale. For beneath each number was a person, with aspirations, a family, a past, and dreams for the future. Dreams snuffed out in the icy plains of Siberia.

Archival excavations, piecing together fragments from various sources, have shed light on some specifics. During the harshest years, especially during the Second World War when supplies were constrained and the demand for production was highest, death was a constant companion for the inmates. Malnutrition was rampant, and the daily ration of bread – often the only barrier between life and a slow, painful death – was woefully inadequate. Diseases like scurvy, due to vitamin C deficiency, and typhus were common killers. The biting cold, with temperatures often plunging to -50 degrees Celsius, was an ever-present executioner.

Moreover, the nature of the work assigned, often involving mining and construction without proper tools or protective gear, meant accidents were frequent. The rate of industrial accidents in Kolyma was several times higher than the national average, further adding to the grim tally.

What of those who survived the ordeal? They bore the physical and mental scars of their time in the camps. Emaciated figures, haunted eyes, and spirits broken by the relentless machine of the gulag were common sights. Many suffered from post-traumatic stress, a condition not well understood or acknowledged at the time. Their stories, whispered in hushed tones in the dark corners of Soviet society, were testimonies to human resilience and the indomitable will to live.

The cultural and intellectual loss, too, was profound. Many of Kolyma's prisoners were intellectuals, artists, writers, and political figures. Their potential contributions to society, art, and culture were lost in the depths of Kolyma's mines and labor camps. Think of the unwritten books, the unpainted canvases, the unsung songs; the world was robbed of these in the frozen wastes of Siberia.

In the aftermath of the Stalin era, as the gulag system was gradually wound down, the focus was on rebuilding and moving forward. The Soviet authorities, not eager to highlight the darkest chapters of their reign, were not forthcoming with accurate data. Many records were lost, destroyed, or remain classified to this day. The true scale of the human tragedy may never be fully known.

However, in the 1990s, as glasnost took root and the Soviet Union dissolved, efforts were intensified to understand the scale of the tragedy. Research institutions and historians delved deep into archives, personal testimonies, and the few remaining official records to stitch together the human story of Kolyma.

The narrative that emerged was one of immense suffering but also of resilience. The human cost of Kolyma is a testament to the extremes of human cruelty but also to the spirit's ability to endure, resist, and, ultimately, to bear witness.

As we reflect on the numbers and the stories behind them, it's crucial to remember that history isn't just about grand events or overarching narratives. It's also about the individual, the personal, the singular stories that, together, form the mosaic of our shared past.

CHAPTER 22:

Religion, Faith, and Spiritual Resistance

Amidst the permafrost plains and desolate stretches of Kolyma, in an environment where man wrestled daily against nature and its own cruelty, faith flourished. It was a quiet, desperate kind of faith; one nurtured in secret corners and within whispered prayers. The Communist regime's relentless crackdown on religious beliefs did not extinguish the quiet flame of spirituality; instead, it forced it to adapt, transform, and sometimes even intensify.

The Bolshevik Revolution had, from its inception, been wary of organized religion. Churches were seen as bourgeois institutions that promoted outdated, oppressive ideas. Clerics were derided as the "servants of the Tsar and bourgeoisie." To the new Soviet state, religion was not just superstitious; it was anti-revolutionary, an obstacle to creating the ideal socialist citizen. Measures were quickly implemented to secularize society. Churches were confiscated, monasteries shut down, and religious teaching prohibited in schools. Clergy members who resisted faced imprisonment or worse.

But faith, one learns, is not so easily dispelled. Especially not in the throes of suffering.

Within the confines of Kolyma, as in many other parts of the Gulag system, the camp inmates sought solace wherever they could find it. And for many, this solace was found in the divine. What is fascinating is not just that faith persisted, but how it evolved, amalgamated, and often intertwined with the brutal reality of camp life.

We might consider, for instance, the clandestine religious gatherings that took place in the barracks. Under the cover of night, in the darkness lit only by a single candle or lantern, prisoners would gather. Some were former priests or monks, others merely devout believers, and still, others who'd rediscovered their faith amidst hardship. These spiritual leaders would recall, from memory, fragments of liturgy, hymns, and scripture. Communion might be served with crumbs of bread, symbolizing the body of Christ. Confessions were whispered, absolutions given, and hope was kindled. All this was done in profound secrecy; discovery would mean severe punishment.

This rekindling of faith wasn't limited to Christianity. Jews observed the Sabbath and other religious rituals in hiding, Muslims practiced their daily prayers away from prying eyes, and Buddhists sought to find inner peace through quiet meditation. Religious diversity was, despite the shared suffering, quietly celebrated. Tales abound of Muslim prisoners sharing their scant food with Christian inmates during Christian fasts, and vice versa during Ramadan. It was a testament to the innate human capacity to find commonality, even in belief, during the direst of circumstances.

The physical manifestations of faith were often stripped away, but the essence persisted. Rosaries were confiscated, but prisoners counted prayers on their fingers. Icons were prohibited, but believers drew them in the snow or etched them on the icy walls of their barracks with their breath. The absence of religious texts led many to rely on memory; verses of the Quran, Bible, or other sacred scriptures were passed down orally, and in the absence of precise memory, often took on a poetic quality of their own.

Religion also offered a lens through which prisoners could interpret and cope with their suffering. Many saw their experience in Kolyma as a test, a Jobian trial. Just as Job was tested by God, so too were they. This interpretation offered solace because it framed their suffering within a larger narrative, one that promised eventual redemption and justice.

However, it wasn't all clandestine reverence. The guards and officials, many of whom came from religious backgrounds themselves, often struggled with the juxtaposition of their own beliefs against their roles. Some, in moments of reflection or doubt, would engage in philosophical or theological debates with the more educated prisoners, particularly former priests or monks. These discussions, happening in stolen moments away from the eyes of other officials, highlighted the complexity of the human psyche and the constant search for meaning, even amongst those inflicting suffering.

Moreover, amidst this tapestry of faith and adversity, new forms of spirituality were birthed. Syncretic beliefs, amalgamations of different religious traditions, began to form. These were religions of the Gulag, faiths that drew from multiple traditions to make sense of the unparalleled suffering. They weren't institutionalized, but they were deeply personal. Tales of the Madonna interwoven with Buddhist parables or Islamic teachings merged with Christian saints. This was faith at its most adaptive, reshaping and reforming itself to respond to the direst human conditions.

For some, though, Kolyma and its cruelties tested their faith to the point of obliteration. The constant onslaught of suffering, the death, and the perceived silence of a higher power made belief untenable. They questioned the existence of a divine entity that could allow such horrors. Their crisis of faith was profound, shaking the very core of their being.

Yet, the story of religion in Kolyma isn't one of its demise, but of its tenacity. It's a testament to the enduring human spirit and its search for meaning even in the darkest corners of existence. The icy winds of Siberia couldn't extinguish the flames of belief, hope, and the eternal human quest for the divine.

When the tales of Kolyma are retold, the focus is often on the visible, tangible aspects: the labor, the cold, the death. But intertwined with these narratives is another tale, one that speaks of the intangible, the ethereal. It's a tale that reminds us that even in the darkest nights of the human soul, there is a flicker of light, a whisper of hope, and a quiet prayer ascending towards the heavens.

CHAPTER 23

Ethnicities and Nationalities: Diversity in Suffering

It is a misnomer to envision the Siberian gulags, particularly the numbing depths of Kolyma, as places reserved solely for the Russian dissident or the politically wayward ethnic Russian. Rather, the skeletal fingers of Stalin's terror network reached out, ensnaring a vivid tapestry of ethnicities and nationalities, ensuring that the song of suffering, while uniformly haunting, was sung in a multitude of languages, dialects, and with varying inflections.

The Soviet Union was an empire, vast not only in geography but in the range of its constituent nationalities. As Stalin tightened his grip on every facet of Soviet life, a patchwork quilt of nationalities found themselves in the crosshairs, their fates sealed by real or perceived insubordination, or simply because they were considered strategically problematic. The Arctic confines of Kolyma bore witness to this grim spectrum of humanity.

Among the first to be branded as enemies were the kulaks, or wealthy peasants, from Ukraine. Post the orchestrated Holodomor famine, any potential resistance needed stifling. Ukrainians, for their earlier bids for independence, were subjected to forced collectivization.

Those resisting or voicing dissent were branded enemies and dispatched to Siberia. Kolyma's camps absorbed these souls, who clung to their traditions and languages, their whispered lullabies standing testament in the biting cold.

But the Ukrainians were by no means the sole tenants of this icy purgatory. The Baltics, having been annexed by the Soviet Union during World War II, brought with them Lithuanians, Latvians, and Estonians. Their crime? A desire for independence, a dream for which many had already fought in the earlier decades. The Soviets, however, viewed their nationalism as a direct affront to the state's ideology. Intellectuals, political leaders, and even common folk from these regions found themselves ensnared in the treacherous net cast by the NKVD.

Kolyma's winds also echoed with the sorrowful tunes of the Caucasus. Chechens and Ingush, deported en masse from their homelands due to their alleged collaboration with Nazi Germany, found the frigid landscape of Kolyma a grotesque contrast to the rugged beauty of their mountainous homes. Accused of treachery, entire families, including children and the elderly, were packed into cattle cars, their destination - the deadly camps of Kolyma.

It was a similar story for the Crimean Tatars. Accused collectively of collaborating with the Nazis, the entire population, without exception, was deported in 1944. Men, women, children, the elderly – none were spared. Many perished en route, while those who survived the torturous journey faced the inhospitable conditions of the Siberian hinterlands. Their rich cultural tapestry, full of tales from the Crimean shores, was woven instead against the bleak backdrop of the Kolyma camps.

Koreans, too, found themselves tragically misplaced. Originally settled in the Far East, they were the first nationality to be deported by the Soviet Union in the 1930s, largely due to the Soviet leadership's paranoia over Japan's imperial ambitions. Thus, even before the camps of Kolyma reached their zenith of infamy, Koreans had already tasted its cold bitterness.

The Volga Germans, descendants of Germans who had settled in Russia during the time of Catherine the Great, were another group that bore the brunt of Stalin's ethnic cleansings. With the Nazi invasion, Stalin's suspicion of the Volga Germans' loyalties intensified, and the entire community was deported to the east. Many found themselves in the unforgiving terrains of Kolyma, their German refrains and dialects adding another layer to the region's tragic linguistic tapestry.

It wasn't just those from the European frontiers of the Soviet Union that were thrust into this abyss. The Kalmyks, Buddhists and the only people in Europe to follow the tenets of Buddhism, were also victims of this era. Accused of collaboration with the Germans during their occupation of the Kalmyk ASSR, they were subsequently subjected to one of the most ruthless deportations, with a significant number ending up in Kolyma.

These ethnic groups, each with its history, traditions, and languages, became unwilling inhabitants of Kolyma's bleak expanse. Their diverse backgrounds only intensified the shared experience of suffering. While they came from different corners of the vast Soviet empire, in Kolyma, their identities blurred into one - prisoners, victims of an unforgiving regime that saw diversity as a threat.

Yet, despite the adversity, the spirit of these varied ethnicities wasn't easily subdued. Oral histories, whispered tales of yore, songs, and traditions passed down generations were shared, even in the face of death. In doing so, these prisoners ensured their cultures would not be forgotten. An unintended consequence of the mass deportations and incarcerations was the mingling of traditions and stories, creating a unique blend of shared memories.

What's profoundly moving is not just the scale of the tragedy but the rich diversity of those who suffered. The camps of Kolyma were a microcosm of the Soviet Union itself, a tragic representation of its vastness and variety. The indomitable spirit of these diverse groups, their ability to hold onto their cultural identities even in the face of unparalleled adversity, stands as a poignant testament to the resilience of the human spirit.

As we reflect on the vast tapestry of cultures that found themselves in Kolyma's icy grasp, it's essential to remember that while their experiences were shared, each group brought with it a unique history, a distinct legacy of traditions, and a rich array of memories. And in the end, it was perhaps these very memories, stories, and traditions that provided a glimmer of hope, a fleeting respite, amid the unrelenting desolation of Kolyma.

CHAPTER 24

Life After the Gulag

In the wake of the heaviest snowstorm, as the wintry blizzards gave way to the spring thaw, those who emerged from the frostbitten bowels of Kolyma also experienced a metamorphosis of their own. They were no longer mere numbers, calculated losses on a sprawling bureaucracy's cold list; they were now, once again, men and women – survivors, bearers of scars both seen and unseen. But what, exactly, did 'life after the Gulag' entail? Could it ever return to what it once was, or was it merely an exercise in forging a new existence from the shards of the old?

It is vital to understand that the road to freedom, even when the gates of the Gulag clanged shut behind them, was never a straightforward journey. It was interspersed with checkpoints, scrutinies, and suspicions. These were not, after all, merely men and women who had served their time, but individuals who bore the indelible stamp of the Gulag, marking them, to many, as potential dissidents, rebels, and outcasts.

Upon their release, many former prisoners found themselves deprived of civil rights. While not universally applicable, several were stripped of their Soviet citizenship and rendered 'stateless.' They were released, yes, but into a land where they officially didn't belong. Their place in society was at the fringe, existing, but not truly belonging. Their voting rights were removed, and for many, the mere act of securing employment became a Sisyphean task. The stigma attached to having been in Kolyma was a mark hard to wash away.

Then, there were those who, officially, had their rights reinstated but found society unwilling to accept them back. Tales of former inmates being denied jobs, ostracized by neighbors, or even shunned by family members are all too common in the annals of post-Gulag literature. It seems the Siberian frost had a way of lingering in their bones, setting them apart from their fellow citizens.

Many survivors relocated, seeking anonymity in the vast expanse of the Soviet Union. These internal migrations, sometimes voluntary and sometimes enforced, had the effect of dispersing the population of former Kolyma inmates. It was, in many ways, a second exile – a journey away from the haunting memories of the Gulag to cities like Tashkent or Yerevan. But memories, especially those etched in pain and suffering, have a way of following one, irrespective of the geographical distances covered.

Moreover, the post-Kolyma era brought with it a different sort of incarceration for many: the imprisonment of silence. The state's narrative, a monolithic version of events where the Gulags were either downplayed or justified as a necessity, loomed large. Attempts to counter this narrative, to share personal stories of suffering and endurance, were often met with state censorship or even persecution. The state's machinery, which had once confined them physically, now sought to confine their narratives, their truths.

But, as with any large system, there were cracks. Through these, stories of survival seeped out. Samizdat literature, or self-published works, began to circulate covertly. These handwritten or typed accounts, passed secretly from one reader to another, acted as a testament to the human spirit's resilience. They were acts of defiance, a way of ensuring that the memories of Kolyma, and the countless other Gulags, were not whitewashed from history.

Economically, the situation was equally challenging. For those who managed to find employment, their salaries were often meager, and they found themselves at the lowest rungs of the professional ladder, irrespective of their qualifications or past achievements. There were tales of professors turning janitors, of artists hauling coal. The narrative of the downtrodden rising through sheer determination exists, but it's not the norm. For most, the struggle was constant, the victories small and hard-won.

Over time, there were initiatives to 'rehabilitate' the survivors of the Gulags. The 1950s saw the Soviet state begin to exonerate many of those who had been unjustly imprisoned, but this process was neither swift nor comprehensive. For some, it came too late; for others, the scars were too deep to be salved by a mere state decree.

It is essential to mention the families of these survivors. Children, who had grown up with the shadow of their parents' incarceration looming over them, often found themselves labeled, stigmatized by association. Marriages strained under the weight of shared traumas, of memories too painful to articulate. Reintegration into society was not merely a personal journey; it was a collective one, undertaken by families and, sometimes, entire communities.

Yet, amidst this vast tapestry of suffering and endurance, tales of hope persist. There were stories of communities coming together, of former inmates forming support groups, of the indomitable human spirit forging paths where none existed. There were accounts of love blossoming in the most unlikely of places, of families torn apart by the Gulags finding their way back to each other, of art and literature acting as a balm for the most searing of wounds.

In concluding this exploration of life post-Kolyma, one is reminded of the intricate mosaic that history often is. There are shades of gray, of white, of the darkest black. The survivors of Kolyma, with their myriad tales of endurance, suffering, hope, and rebirth, add to this mosaic, ensuring that while the Siberian frosts may have receded, the memories they left behind remain indelibly etched in the annals of time.

CHAPTER 25

The Thaw: The Beginning of the End for Kolyma

The snows in Siberia thaw slowly. As the layers of frost recede, the land unveils stories preserved in ice, the chilling tales of the past. The same could be said about the political climate of the USSR after the death of Joseph Stalin in 1953. A shift began, subtle at first, then more apparent, like the first trickles of water from melting snow. This period, known to history as the Khrushchev Thaw, was an era marked by a considerable liberalization in the politics, culture, and society of the Soviet Union. It was in this period that the Gulag system, with Kolyma as one of its darkest symbols, began to be dismantled.

The monolithic empire that Stalin had constructed was rooted in the fear of dissent and deviation. But as the Soviet Union emerged from the shadow of his iron grip, change was not just expected—it was inevitable. The winds of change first blew in the 20th Congress of the Communist Party of the Soviet Union in February 1956. Nikita Khrushchev, in a move that shocked both the East and the West, denounced the horrors of Stalin's rule in his secret speech, officially titled "On the Cult of Personality and Its Consequences." He boldly tackled the repressions, mass arrests, and executions of the previous era. While not a complete and detailed disclosure of all atrocities, it laid the groundwork for a transformation in the Soviet system.

Khrushchev's speech was a repudiation of Stalin's methods, and it immediately set off debates within the Communist party. There were hardliners who believed that Stalin's measures, however brutal, were necessary to protect the Soviet state. On the other side, the reformists saw a chance to break away from the oppressive past. But beyond the corridors of power, the revelations, as they trickled down, instigated a more profound introspection amongst the Soviet populace.

Kolyma, with its vast expanse of labor camps, represented the excesses of Stalin's Gulag system. After the dictator's death, the need to maintain such a colossal, brutal, and expensive prison system became untenable. The government, grappling with economic realities and keen to project a more humane image both domestically and abroad, initiated a gradual closure of many of the camps.

Between 1954 and 1957, vast numbers of prisoners, though not all, were released from the Gulags. The closure of the camps wasn't always a systematic process. Some were shut down due to logistical challenges, some due to reduced economic viability, and others were closed as part of the wider policy of de-Stalinization. Kolyma, due to its significant gold mining operations, didn't see an immediate shutdown of all its facilities. However, the manner in which the camps operated began to change. Forced labor was reduced, living conditions improved marginally, and there was a reduction in the scale of brutality. It was an end, not marked by fanfare, but by a silent, begrudging retreat.

However, the dissolution of the camps did not mean an immediate end to the suffering of those who were once imprisoned. Many prisoners, upon release, found themselves in a world vastly different from the one they remembered. Families had been torn apart, homes had been lost, and the stigma of having been a Gulag inmate was not easily shaken off. The state provided minimal assistance, and for many, the freedom they had yearned for was replaced by a new struggle for survival in Soviet society.

The reforms did not stop at the prison gates. The Thaw era brought about significant changes in Soviet literature, arts, and media. The previously enforced doctrines which curtailed any form of expression that deviated from the party line were relaxed. Books that had been previously banned, like Solzhenitsyn's 'One Day in the Life of Ivan Denisovich', which narrated the life inside a labor camp, were now being published. These publications gave the Soviet people, and the world, an intimate glimpse into the conditions of the Gulags.

It's essential to understand that Khrushchev's Thaw wasn't just a benevolent act of a compassionate leader. The USSR, during this period, was going through significant socio-political changes. The Cold War was intensifying, and the race for global influence against the West was on. The memories of Stalin's purges were fresh, and there was a genuine fear that if reforms were not initiated, internal dissent might grow. Moreover, there was an economic dimension. The vast Gulag system was expensive to maintain, and with the focus shifting towards the space race and nuclear armament, resources had to be diverted.

Yet, while the Thaw led to the decline of the Gulag system, it didn't necessarily herald a complete end to political repressions in the Soviet Union. There were crackdowns on dissidents, albeit on a much smaller scale than during Stalin's era. The regime, despite its reforms, remained suspicious of any form of dissent.

The impact of the Thaw on the memory of Kolyma is multifaceted. On the one hand, it opened the doors for narratives from the labor camps to emerge and be discussed. Yet, on the other, the scale of the horror was so vast that the full comprehension of what had transpired in places like Kolyma took time to permeate the national and global consciousness.

The ebb of the tide that was the Khrushchev Thaw revealed the scars on the landscape of the Soviet Union. Kolyma stood as a testament to these scars, a solemn reminder of the limits of human endurance and the depths to which humanity can descend. In the annals of history, places like Kolyma serve as cautionary tales, underscoring the importance of eternal vigilance against the rise of oppressive regimes. The gradual dismantling of the Gulag system during the Thaw was not just the closing of prison gates; it was the opening of a nation's eyes to its own recent, harrowing past.

CHAPTER 26

Kolyma's Legacy in Soviet Literature and Art

In the aftermath of the epochal weight that bore down upon the citizens incarcerated within Kolyma's walls, the scalding memories of that inhospitable land manifested themselves vividly in the arts. The very notion of a frozen wasteland, where suffering was the language and despair, its tune, was fathomlessly deep and vast. But it was this abyss of human suffering that subsequently became a crucible for some of the most profound expressions in Soviet literature and art. Like pressing the heaviest of diamonds, these expressions emerged, unapologetically fierce and clear.

The literature of the period that directly followed Stalin's reign often bore silent testimonies, voices that were once suppressed, now clawing their way into the light. If we turn our gaze, for instance, to the words of Aleksandr Solzhenitsyn, a luminary among those who detailed life in the Gulag, we observe not just narrative, but a haunting illustration of humanity's perseverance. "One Day in the Life of Ivan Denisovich" was more than fiction—it was a raw imprint of memory. Each line captured the leaden cold, the numbing hunger, and the degradation of spirit, transporting the reader directly to the tundra. For many, it wasn't just literature; it was a revelation.

Then there was Varlam Shalamov, whose experiences in Kolyma directly influenced his series of stories collectively titled "Kolyma Tales". Unlike Solzhenitsyn's broader look at the Gulag system, Shalamov took the reader to the frostbitten heart of Kolyma. His narrative was sparse, stark—each word chosen with a precision that cut through the soul. There was no room for embellishment or flowery prose; the truth of Kolyma demanded simplicity.

Yet, it wasn't just the written word that echoed the pain and loss. Visual arts, especially painting, became a medium of poignant reflection. Painters like Nikolai Getman, himself a former Gulag prisoner, took it upon himself to chronicle life in the labor camps. His paintings, often reminiscent of the bleakness captured in the works of earlier Russian artists like Ilya Repin, presented the desolation and dehumanization of camp life. The furrowed brows, the lifeless eyes, the gaunt faces against the blinding white of snow and the oppressive weight of the timber they carried—it wasn't just paint on canvas. It was a cry, a plea, a remembrance.

Art and literature of this period had a singular mission: to ensure that the memory of the Gulag, and especially Kolyma, remained an indelible scar on the face of Soviet history. These works were not merely reactionary or borne out of a need for catharsis, but they were a bold act of resistance against the machinery that would have these tales buried, forgotten.

In the realm of films, the Gulag narrative took a slightly nuanced approach. A particular standout in this domain was the 1991 film "Lost in Siberia", directed by Alexander Mitta. Set in Kolyma it tells the tale of a British archaeologist, engaged in an excavation in the northern stretches of Iran, who inadvertently draws the attention of the Soviet intelligence, mistakenly being identified as an American undercover agent. Whisked away to Moscow and subsequently dispatched to an isolated Siberian detention center, he grapples with retaining his human spirit amidst the brutality of the camp's overseers and the moral decay exhibited by seasoned convicts, who are incarcerated alongside those imprisoned for their political beliefs.

Western writers, also tried to grasp the haunting resonance of Kolyma. Notable mentions must be made of "Gulag: A History" by Anne Applebaum and "The Great Terror" by Robert Conquest. Both works, although from a non-native perspective, sought to understand and relay the depths of human endurance, the cost of political fanaticism, and the resilience of the human spirit, even when shackled in chains and cloaked in despair.

Dance, an art form that thrives on visceral expression, could not remain untouched by the Kolyma experience. Choreographers like Boris Eifman presented modern ballet performances that drew inspiration from the Gulag memories. In one such memorable performance, dancers portrayed the anguished souls of the prisoners, their bodies bending, twisting, and turning, in a vivid representation of their tormented existence. The stark stage, illuminated only by dim lights casting long, eerie shadows, mirrored the hopelessness of the camps, while the haunting music emphasized their pain and longing.

This legacy, woven intricately through the fabric of Soviet arts, was more than a reflection—it was a lesson. Each pen scratch, brush stroke, and dance move served as a reminder that history, when forgotten or brushed aside, has a haunting way of repeating itself. Artists ensured that the memory of Kolyma wasn't merely a chapter in a history book, but an ever-present cautionary tale.

One could argue that these expressions were more than just art—they were the very essence of memory, and memory, as history has shown time and again, is the most potent weapon against tyranny. While regimes and rulers may try to control or suppress voices, the soul finds its own language, its own form of expression. For the inmates of Kolyma, and for the generations that followed, art and literature became that undying voice.

As the sun sets on this chapter of history, the dark silhouette of Kolyma looms large. But in its shadow, the defiant spirit of its inmates, echoed through the arts, stands even taller, ensuring that the world neither forgets nor forgives the horror that unfolded in that frozen wasteland. And in that assurance, in that memory, lies the indomitable spirit of humanity—forever resilient, forever enduring.

CHAPTER 27

The Road to Rehabilitation: Accepting the Past

Even as the ice of the political climate began to thaw, the memory of Kolyma, carved deep in the minds of those who survived it and on the pages of hushed Soviet records, refused to melt away. The fading, yet indelible scar it left on the landscape of Soviet history stood as a testament to the harrowing past, demanding recognition, redress, and remembrance.

The Soviet Union, under the rising influence of Khrushchev, heralded a departure from the era of extreme repression and secrecy of the Stalin years. Though Kolyma's camps had largely ceased operations, a pertinent question lingered: How would a nation address such profound internal wounds? The process of delving into, understanding, and atoning for Kolyma's dark history would be tortuous, marked by both denial and acceptance.

In the immediate aftermath of the worst excesses of the Gulag system, the Soviet government's initial approach was marked by a reticence to fully acknowledge the scope of the atrocities. The initial discourse was characterized less by outright denial but more by a strategic silence. The vast machinery of the Soviet bureaucracy, which once meticulously documented arrests and camp logistics, now seemed to cast a shroud of obfuscation over this harrowing chapter.

But as Khrushchev's leadership paved the way for a period of de-Stalinization, the official narrative began to change. The Secret Speech of 1956, delivered by Khrushchev at the 20th Party Congress, stands out as a landmark moment. While not a public mea culpa, this internal denunciation of Stalin's purges marked the beginning of a slow, hesitant process of national introspection.

Over time, as the reigns of subsequent Soviet leaders unfolded, the strategy of dealing with the Kolyma legacy oscillated between cautious acknowledgment and a return to reticence. It was a delicate dance, with leaders wary of destabilizing the nation's sense of self or the Communist Party's stronghold by fully unearthing the grim skeletons of the past.

However, societal pressures were mounting. Survivors, many of whom were reintegrating into society, began to narrate their tales. Although their stories were not always welcome, and many faced skepticism, disbelief, or even reprisals, the truth had a way of seeping through the cracks of official narratives.

By the 1980s, the atmosphere in the Soviet Union was again changing. The era of Glasnost, introduced by Mikhail Gorbachev, advocated for increased openness and transparency in governance. This climate of relative liberalization provided the much-needed impetus for a deeper acknowledgment of the tragedies of Kolyma.

This was not solely a top-down process. Grassroots movements, bolstered by the personal narratives of survivors and investigative works of committed historians and journalists, began to shape the collective consciousness. Prominent figures like Aleksandr Solzhenitsyn, with his magnum opus "The Gulag Archipelago," played a pivotal role in not just domestic discourse but also in illuminating the horrors of the Gulag system to the global community.

As the Soviet Union approached its eventual dissolution in 1991, the path to rehabilitation and compensation became more tangible. The Russian Federation, emerging from the ashes of the Soviet regime, was confronted with the weighty task of addressing its past. Under Boris Yeltsin's presidency, the 1990s saw a slew of legal and legislative efforts aimed at rehabilitating the victims of political repression. Laws were enacted to restore civil rights, offer compensation, and, crucially, to legally recognize the injustices meted out by the Soviet regime.

While these legal measures were significant, they were not devoid of challenges. The sheer scale of the task, encompassing decades of repression and millions of victims, posed logistical problems. How would compensation be determined? How could the myriad experiences of suffering, ranging from summary executions to prolonged detention, be categorized for redress? And, crucially, how would the Russian state, grappling with its own economic and political challenges in the post-Soviet transition, finance these compensations?

Moreover, the legal and bureaucratic processes of rehabilitation often came up against the very real human challenge of memory and evidence. Many victims, having faced the horrors of Kolyma decades earlier, found it challenging to produce the necessary documentation to validate their experiences, given the Soviet regime's prior efforts at obfuscation.

Beyond legislation, the path to accepting the past also meandered through the realms of education and public discourse. Efforts were made to integrate the truth of Kolyma and the broader Gulag system into school curricula, ensuring that newer generations grew up with a more unvarnished understanding of their nation's history.

Yet, this journey was not linear. With the turn of the century and under the leadership of Vladimir Putin, a noted resurgence of nationalistic sentiments saw a nuanced, sometimes ambivalent approach to the Soviet past. While the horrors of the Gulag, including Kolyma, were not denied outright, there was a discernible shift towards emphasizing the Soviet Union's achievements, especially its role in the Second World War.

For the survivors of Kolyma and their descendants, this oscillating national stance was a reminder of the fragility of memory and the importance of vigilant remembrance. Their personal narratives, shared in whispered tales, penned memoirs, or captured in art, formed a resilient tapestry of truth, a bulwark against the tides of revisionism.

In conclusion, the road to rehabilitation, to acknowledging and atoning for Kolyma's haunting legacy, was neither smooth nor straightforward. It was a path fraught with political considerations, societal debates, and the very human struggle to confront uncomfortable truths. But it was a journey the Russian Federation, inheriting the weighty legacy of the Soviet past, had to undertake, not just for the sake of its victims but for the soul of the nation itself. In the mosaic of memory, the pieces depicting Kolyma, dark and chilling, remain crucial, reminding Russia and the world of the depths to which humanity can sink and the imperative to ensure history doesn't repeat itself.

CHAPTER 28

Kolyma Today: Tourism, Memorials, and Memory

Few landscapes possess a melancholy more profound than Kolyma's vast, icy plains, whose bleak horizon has been inscribed with decades of human suffering. One might anticipate such a place to be shrouded permanently in the shadows of its past, much as Pompeii remains in ashen stasis beneath Vesuvius's bellicose silhouette. But time, as it does, moves forward, often in ways that history's most ardent guardians find unsettling.

Today's Kolyma is not the frozen wasteland into which countless souls vanished during the era of Stalin's purges. Nature, with its habit of renewal, has seen to the blossoming of life where death once prevailed. The resilient Siberian flora, piercing through the thawed permafrost, seems intent on proving the inexorability of life. Yet, it is not nature alone that seeks to reclaim this land, but also those humans who recognize its rich tapestry of history and memory.

With the disintegration of the Soviet Union, the hitherto iron curtains concealing numerous state secrets began to part. Kolyma, once a forbidden territory, its very name invoking dread, slowly opened its gates to the outside world. As the archives revealed their hoarded truths, there emerged a growing realization that the memory of the victims deserved a fitting commemoration.

In an era of booming global tourism, where battlefields like Verdun and concentration camps like Auschwitz have been transformed into places of memory, it was perhaps inevitable that Kolyma would find itself on the itinerary of the historically curious. The decision to admit tourists to such sites is always fraught, tiptoeing on the line between education and voyeurism.

The challenge has been to educate without sensationalizing; to invoke empathy without leaning into spectacle. And in the vastness of Kolyma, creating a meaningful narrative is more akin to curating a country than a museum. How does one bring into perspective such a sprawling canvas of suffering?

A few of the former Gulag sites have been preserved as somber memorials, their rusted structures, half-devoured by the elements, standing as skeletal testimonies to past atrocities. The silence there is haunting. With no need for embellishment, the remnants of the camps — barren watchtowers, dilapidated barracks, chains now rigid with rust — speak volumes to visitors. Such spaces are stark reminders of George Santayana's often-quoted adage: "Those who cannot remember the past are condemned to repeat it."

In stark contrast stands the Kolyma Highway, or the 'Road of Bones', named for the remains of the forced laborers purportedly used in its construction. This road has taken on a new identity, attracting intrepid motorists from around the world. They traverse its lengths, marveling at the desolation, perhaps without grasping the full weight of the tragedies buried beneath the surface.

Yet, it's not merely the physical remnants that bring the past alive. Several local initiatives seek to bridge the historical chasm by sharing oral histories, passed down generations, about life during the Gulag era. These first-hand accounts, offered by descendants of the victims, provide a personal connection that static exhibits or preserved sites might lack. There's a rawness to these tales, an immediacy, even if second-hand, that brings the chilling past into sharp focus.

But perhaps the most significant embodiment of memory is the annual "Memory Watch" event. Instituted in the 1990s, this event sees descendants of the victims, joined by history enthusiasts and volunteers, undertaking treks across Kolyma, retracing the footsteps of the incarcerated. Along their journey, they restore neglected graves, erect memorials, and, above all, ensure that the memories of those who perished in this icy wasteland remain alive.

This juxtaposition of the old and the new, the grim past and the hopeful present, is best seen in the town of Magadan, once the administrative center overseeing the network of Kolyma camps. Here, modern buildings rub shoulders with Soviet-era structures, creating an architectural mosaic that mirrors Russia's own tumultuous history. The town's most striking feature, however, is the "Mask of Sorrow" — a colossal monument dedicated to the memory of the victims. The sculpture, depicting a face with tears streaming down, is a solemn guardian of memory, watching over the town and its inhabitants.

Yet, as time marches forward, there remains the pressing question of how such memories will be preserved for future generations. With each passing year, the direct links to the traumatic events of the past — the survivors, the guards, the direct witnesses — are fading away, leaving behind second and third-hand accounts. The danger, as always, lies in the narrative being sanitized or diluted, detached from its harrowing emotions.

There's an inherent tension in memorializing trauma on such a scale. On one hand, there's a need to remember, to acknowledge, and to learn. On the other, there's the risk of commercializing sorrow, turning it into a marketable experience. The path that Kolyma treads in the coming decades will determine how it navigates this tension. For now, amidst the icy winds and desolate landscapes, the memories persist, echoing the tales of a past that the world must never forget.

CHAPTER 29

Comparisons and Parallels: Kolyma in a Global Context

A cross the vast span of the twentieth century, dark clouds periodically obscured the sunlit arcs of human progress. These were times when fear and suspicion dimmed hopes, and societies erected walls, not just of brick and mortar, but of ideological certitude. Each instance was unique, yet bound by a common, chilling thread of human suffering, with Kolyma being one of its darkest expressions. To place the atrocities of Kolyma into a broader context, we must cast our gaze beyond the peripheries of the Soviet Union, onto a world stage where other oppressive regimes and camps etched their sinister footprints.

The echoes of Kolyma reverberate most eerily when juxtaposed with the tales from the Third Reich's concentration camps. Nazi Germany's solution to political dissidents, "undesirables," and the horror of its racial cleansing found its monstrous embodiment in places like Auschwitz, Dachau, and Treblinka. While Hitler's animus was profoundly tied to racial and ethnic cleansing, Stalin's wrath, though occasionally ethnically directed, primarily focused on political purification. The Nazi concentration camps, with their meticulously planned extermination methods, were distinct from the Gulag system's primary intent: forced labor. Still, the torturous existence, the capricious violence, and the vast machinery of oppression, evoke disturbing parallels.

Moving east, another shade of this macabre spectrum became visible in Cambodia during the 1970s. The Khmer Rouge, led by Pol Pot, sought to create an agrarian utopia by eradicating all traces of urbanity and modernity. The Tuol Sleng prison, originally a high school, became a symbol of the extreme lengths to which ideologies can push humanity. Here, intellectuals, professionals, and even those with mild affiliations to the old regime were subjected to brutal interrogations, torture, and ultimately, death. Like Kolyma's haunting freeze, Tuol Sleng became a chilling testament to the suffering one ideology could inflict upon its people.

Venturing further to the Far East, the tribulations faced by those in China during Mao Zedong's Cultural Revolution provide another page in this tome of oppression. Mao's intent to preserve 'true' Communist ideology led to purges, public humiliations, forced displacements, and a broad spectrum of human rights abuses. Thousands were sent to the Laogai, the Chinese system of labor camps, where forced labor, indoctrination, and harsh conditions echoed the brutalities of Kolyma. Yet, while Mao's campaign was driven by a desire to cleanse the party and society of 'capitalist' elements, the scale and randomness of the violence and its focus on the cultural and intellectual elite draw lines connecting it to the experiences in Kolyma.

The South African apartheid system, with its intent to maintain white supremacy, spawned a range of detention facilities, like the notorious Robben Island. While the primary intent here was segregation and suppression, the human cost, borne primarily by the black and non-white population, was stark. Like the intellectuals in Kolyma, many of South Africa's brightest minds, including Nelson Mandela, endured years of forced labor, isolation, and discrimination in these prisons.

Similarly, Latin America during the Cold War era, particularly in nations such as Chile and Argentina, bore witness to its own set of oppressions. Dictatorships, often with tacit or direct support from superpowers, established detention centers, and clandestine prisons where perceived opponents were tortured, disappeared, or brutally executed. Just as Kolyma saw entire swathes of the population deemed as 'traitors', in Latin America, being a student, an artist, or merely a vocal individual could place you in the crosshairs of the regime.

Each of these instances, though distinctive in their origin, nature, and scale, share haunting parallels with Kolyma. What is it, one wonders, that drives societies, across times and continents, to establish these epicenters of misery?

Perhaps it is the idea of 'purification', a notion that views societies as organisms that must be cleansed of 'impurities' for the larger good. This belief, when combined with unchecked power and an absence of accountability, breeds spaces like Kolyma. Moreover, the creation of an 'other', whether it's based on political ideology, race, religion, or any other divisive measure, justifies, at least in the minds of the oppressors, the establishment of these dark sanctums.

It's also worth noting that each of these oppressive systems operated within a framework of bureaucratic dehumanization. The vast machinery of the state, with its paperwork, procedures, and protocols, made it possible for individuals to absolve themselves of personal responsibility. The tormentor in the camp, the guard at the prison gate, the bureaucrat behind the desk – each became a cog in a machine, enabling atrocities while maintaining a distance from their moral implications.

In drawing these parallels, it is essential to tread with caution. Each instance of mass oppression is embedded within its specific historical, political, and social context. A comparison is not intended to equate, but rather to underline common themes and warn humanity of the dark corridors it can tread when fear supersedes reason.

As we step back and observe the harrowing tapestry of the twentieth century, Kolyma emerges not as an isolated blot but as part of a pattern. A grim reminder of the depths to which humanity can plummet, yes, but also a testament to the human spirit's resilience, which, time and again, has managed to rise, heal, and even, against all odds, hope.

CHAPTER 30

Remembering Kolyma - Why We Must Never Forget

History has an uncanny habit of whispering its tales, not in the broad daylight of noon, but in the delicate twilights of dawn and dusk, where memories are faint, yet haunting. So it is with Kolyma, a name that, for many, emerges from the shadows of the past with a frosty chill and an indelible mark of pain and suffering. The question remains: why is it so essential, so pivotal, to remember?

Recall, if you will, the vast expanse of Siberia – a formidable stretch of wilderness that bore silent witness to one of the most chilling episodes of human history. Kolyma was not an aberration, a stray incident on the timeline of the Soviet Union. It was an institutionalized horror, meticulously planned, and ruthlessly executed. Yet, while the hard earth and the frigid winds of Siberia might try to erase the footprints of those who suffered, the onus of remembrance falls on us.

But why, one may ask, should the generations of today burden themselves with the memories of yesteryears? The past is past, isn't it?

Consider this: human memory is the custodian of identity. Without it, we're but shells of existence. When a chapter as significant as Kolyma is left out of this memory, an essential part of our identity as humanity is obliterated. By remembering, we safeguard against the selective amnesia that often paves the way for history's ugly repetitions.

The trauma of Kolyma, the vast infrastructure of pain, wasn't an isolated occurrence. All across the world, there were analogous systems of persecution: the concentration camps of Nazi Germany, the Killing Fields of Cambodia, the internment camps for Japanese-Americans during World War II. While the specific circumstances, the ideologies behind them, and the scale might differ, they all speak to an underlying thread - the terrifying extents to which humanity can go, given a potent mix of fear, power, and dehumanization.

Yet, while acknowledging the universality of such horrors, it's essential to appreciate the singularity of each episode. Each had its unique cocktail of dread, its particular face of cruelty. In the case of Kolyma, it was the juxtaposition of natural and man-made adversities – the biting cold and the punishing labor; the isolation of Siberia and the absence of hope; the vastness of the landscape and the confinement of the soul.

Memory also has an enlightening aspect. The camps of Kolyma serve as a lens to understand the wider geopolitics of the era. The Cold War, the iron curtain, the ideological tussles between the West and the Soviet bloc – they weren't just macro-events played on the world stage. They had profound micro-impacts, lived daily by thousands in places like Kolyma. In remembering, we gain deeper insights into these intersections of the personal and the political.

But perhaps the most compelling argument for remembrance lies in the realm of ethics. Remembering is an act of posthumous justice. The vast majority of those who bore the brunt of Kolyma's cruelty never got a chance to tell their tales. Their voices were silenced, first by the brutal regime and then by the icy clutches of death. By actively remembering, we allow these voiceless souls a chance at testimony. In this act of collective memory, we recognize their suffering, their sacrifices, and the profound injustice meted out to them.

Moreover, this act of remembering isn't just about looking back. It's also about looking forward. Memory is a guiding light for the future. In a world that continues to grapple with intolerance, extremism, and authoritarianism, the memories of Kolyma serve as a cautionary tale. They remind us of the dire consequences of unchecked power, of the perils of turning a blind eye to the marginalized, and of the importance of preserving the sanctity of every human life.

Remembrance, however, is not without its challenges. The farther we move from an event, the easier it becomes to distort, dilute, or even deny it. Skeptics might raise questions about the veracity of accounts, about the scale of atrocities, about the intent behind them. These voices of doubt, while occasionally stemming from genuine academic inquiry, often have more nefarious origins. They aim to rewrite history, to sanitize it, to fit it into convenient narratives. Against such attempts, collective memory stands as a bulwark. In it lies the strength of countless testimonies, the weight of undeniable evidence, and the power of truth.

As we embark on this journey of memory, we must tread with care. For memory, while powerful, is also fragile. It can be easily swayed by emotions, by biases, by the imperfections of human recall. Our remembrance must be anchored in evidence, in testimonies, in rigorous scholarship. It must be a delicate balance between the empathy of the heart and the scrutiny of the mind.

In conclusion, the story of Kolyma is not just a dark chapter in the annals of the Soviet Union. It is a testament to human endurance, to the indomitable spirit that even the harshest adversities couldn't crush. It is a chronicle of darkness, but also of sparks – sparks of resistance, of hope, of humanity. And as we stand, looking back at this intricate tapestry of pain and perseverance, one thing is clear – we must remember. For in remembrance lies the promise of a world more just, more humane, more compassionate. In the words of George Santayana, "Those who cannot remember the past are condemned to repeat it." Let us not be condemned.

Our Gift to You: Free eBooks Every Week

Dear reader,

As you journey through the annals of history with Hourglass History, we're both humbled and delighted to be your chosen guide. It's a path that we tread together, discovering stories and legacies that have shaped our world.

In the spirit of furthering this voyage of discovery, we've crafted a special offer for our dedicated readers: **Freebie Fridays**. By signing up to our Freebie Friday email list, you will receive just one email each week containing at least one free eBook from Hourglass History.

All we kindly ask in return? After you've delved into the pages and immersed yourself in the tales of yesteryears, please consider leaving us a review on Amazon. Your insights, thoughts, and feedback not only help us refine our offerings but also guide fellow readers on their own historical journeys.

Here's our promise to you:

1. **Quality Over Quantity:** Every book you receive will be one of our full-length books that we normally sell at our full prices.

2. **Privacy is Paramount:** We hold your trust in the highest regard. Rest assured, your details will remain confidential, always.

3. **No Unwanted Distractions:** Our communications will be limited to our one "Freebie Fridays" email each week. No spam. Ever.

4. **Freedom to Choose:** While we'd love to have you with us forever, should you decide to walk different paths, unsubscribing is simple and instant.

To be part of this unique journey, simply sign up at Hourglass History Freebie Fridays (https://hourglasshistory.com/freebie-fridays/), or scan the following QR code:

Your first free eBook is just a Friday away.

Beyond the Pages: Your Part in the Story

Hello dear reader,

First and foremost, thank you. By journeying with us through the frozen landscapes and harrowing tales of "Kolyma: The Frozen Hell of Stalin's Siberian Gulags," you've not just read a book - you've become part of its ever-evolving story.

Our shared expedition through the pages might have concluded, but there's a continuation to this narrative where you play a crucial role. Each page you've turned, every story that's resonated with you, is part of a broader conversation. A conversation about the importance of history, of shared memories, and of lessons learned.

Now, if this book struck a chord with you, there's a simple yet impactful way you can help: leave a review on Amazon. It may seem like a small action, but each review offers fellow readers insights into the value and relevance of these stories. Moreover, your feedback aids in bringing this tale of resilience, courage, and humanity to a broader audience.

Reviews don't just influence potential readers, but they breathe life into stories, ensuring they don't fade into obscurity. Your voice, added to the chorus of others, amplifies the message and reach of this book.

No need for long paragraphs or eloquent language (unless that's your thing!). Just a few honest words about your experience reading "Kolyma: The Frozen Hell of Stalin's Siberian Gulags" will do wonders.

Remember, by sharing your thoughts, you're doing more than just giving feedback. You're championing history, supporting the preservation of memories, and perhaps most importantly, you're reminding everyone that we must look back to move forward with wisdom.

So, if you've got a moment, please consider heading over to Amazon and dropping a few lines. Your words might just be the beacon guiding another reader towards this historical voyage.

Thank you once more for being a cherished part of this narrative. Here's to many more shared stories and lessons!